Grandmagreat's Storytime

Grandmagreat's Storytime

TikTok's Grandma
with More Than
Three Million TikTok Grandchildren

Sharon Barber,
aka Grandmagreat

Cover photo by Maddy Barber Photography
Cover design by Victorine Lieske
Author note photo by Matthew West
Illustrations by Izzy Peterson and Nancy Peterson
Interior print design and layout by Marny K. Parkin
Ebook design and layout by Marny K. Parkin

Published by GGSTTT, LLC

ISBN 979-8-9910341-0-4 print
ISBN 979-8-9910341-1-1 ebook

Contents

Poetry

"Simply Delicious" Recipes

Affirmations

I dedicate the Grandmagreat stories to my faithful
TikTok grandchildren, who have made this journey possible.
I dedicate the poetry to my grandchildren, who have inspired me
Throughout their journey from becoming adorable children,
To sensitive and happy adults.

Introduction to the Audiobook

If you're new to the stories of Sharon Barber, or Grandmagreat, as she's known on TikTok, you are in for an amazing experience.

I listen to a lot of audiobooks, and I gotta tell you, it took me a little while to adjust. Grandmagreat has a condition called spasmodic dysphonia, which gives her voice a unique quality that takes some getting used to. Let me tell you what happened to me:

At first, initially, I found it difficult to understand her, it required more concentration to understand her. Her narration is strikingly different. This is a different experience than your typical audiobook.

HOWEVER, after a little effort on my end, I was intrigued. I could tell there was something special here.

After 2 minutes, I was on board. I got it. I could really feel the reality of these stories, that they happened to her.

At 3 minutes, I was hooked. The difficulty of understanding her makes it captivating, fascinating; it adds to the narration. I'm on the edge of my seat, glad to work harder to understand, because I don't want to miss a word.

At 6–7 minutes, I can't get enough. I'm seeing myself listening to this during the day, and feeling a sense of safety and comfort. I get it. This is the kind of safe, grandmotherly storytelling, so incredibly comforting, that we need right now.

Something as seemingly simple as the story of a young girl buying shoes for a quarter from JC Penney, and it's fascinating. I love this stuff.

And her chuckles and laughs are so charming. The actual writing is great, too. I think you've got something really special, here.

If she's got a fan base who is used to how she sounds, they'll eat this up. People who are used to a pro narrator will have to adjust, but will be rewarded for their patience.

—B. J. Harrison
Host of *The Classic Tales Podcast*
Audiobook narrator of 800+ titles
SOVAS, Hear Now, and IAA winner

Preface

~

Storytelling has been a part of my life for as long as I can remember. One of my first memories was sitting with my little friends at recess while telling the story of the Three Bears!

The stories I relate in this book really happened, and I acknowledge that some of these memories have faded somewhat through the years. While I took a bit of literary license in dialogue or minor details (anyone would be hard pressed to remember a conversation they had over 70 years ago), the themes and lessons of each story are accurate. Each poem is my own creation as well; many of them inspired by real events I share in this book.

I am grateful for the opportunity of finding and including multi-generational recipes, and my TikTok grandchildren who inspired and contributed to Simply Delicious.

I conclude this book with one of my TikTok fan favorites: Affirmations. I always tell my online grandchildren to "say it and believe it!" Because YOU CAN DO HARD THINGS!

Stories

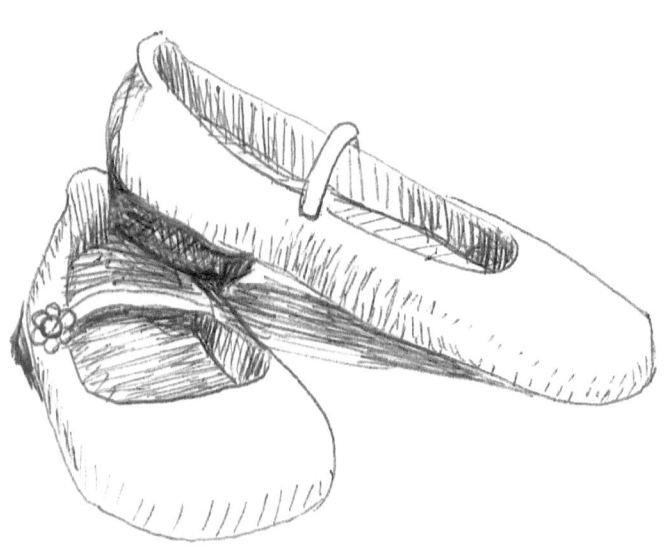

The Yellow Shoes

~

When Grandma pulled her magic bag out of the hall closet, I always knew I was in for a pleasant surprise. Today she had looked at my feet, and her mouth gaped open as it always did when she was about to reveal something that needed to be listened to. I was all ears as she looked at my skinny eight-year-old feet. My shoes were clearly too small, as evidenced by the broken-down backs, the imprints of my toes showing through the worn leather, and the scuffs and stains of spending many hours in the outdoors.

"Sweetie," she said, "what are we going to do about getting you some new shoes?" It sounded like a question, but Grandma always had an answer even though she often asked the question. She pulled the magic bag from the deep, dark closet, of which no one was allowed to even take a peek. I stood back, waiting for the magic to take place. The magic bag was actually an old gray army bag she had picked up at a thrift store many years before.

My grandma was shaped like a big bag of giant marshmallows. The dress she often wore had tiny white circles against a bright red background. When she moved around, it was as if those tiny circles were alive and moving. The red color of the dress was the same color of the bright red lipstick she wore that gently seeped into the lines above and below her thin lips. Grandma took especially good care of her appearance despite her sixty-plus years and lack of funds. She acquired her clothes and mine from thrift stores, hand-me-downs, and wherever else she was able to find them. As she became older, she became shakier, and yet still insisted on wearing a little bit of black mascara that always found itself smudged in the creases of her eyelids, which revealed loving, kind, no-nonsense eyes. Those eyes always had a message before any words were ever said. Her thin gray hair was tightly permed and always in place, with a little curl hanging on her wrinkled forehead that she was always trying to fluff back into the rest of her hair.

As far back as I can remember, I don't think I ever saw her wear anything but the same sturdy black shoes with a pair of ankle socks neatly folded. When she dressed up in Sunday best, it was always the same black dress spread evenly over her marshmallow body, and impeccably pressed until she sat down, and the creases showed up in the material. Grandma was kind, loving, generous, clever, spiritual, and she believed anything was possible. Not necessarily perfect . . . but always possible. She proved this time and time again.

Grandma's funds were limited, yet somehow, I never felt like I missed out on anything. I was able to spend a lot of time with her. My mother and father had divorced.

My mother married again; he was a bad man, who simply did not like me. I was the oldest, and I spent most of my time taking care of my four younger brothers and the rest of my free time trying to console my unhealthy and unhappy mother. It was a lot of responsibility for a little lanky girl. Being with my grandma made me happy and gave me the sense I was important and needed.

This day had been especially fun as we had gone early to Bertha's Bakery, which was located just down the street and around the corner from my grandma's big red brick house. We could smell the aroma of the fresh bread baking before we ever came to the door of that tiny neighborhood bakery, which started the bread long before the day had begun. We would step inside to the delicious aroma coming from the oven. Grandma would say to me, "OK, sweetie, take a big whiff of that delicious bread," and she would watch as I breathed in the tantalizing aroma. She would then step to the day-old rack and pick up and pay for a loaf. When we got outside, she would say, "We didn't miss a thing. We got the fresh baked aroma, and now we are going home to enjoy this delicious bread with butter and honey." Grandma would eat a slice or two, and then she would just watch me gobble slice after slice with a smile on her face. This has always been a memory I have cherished.

As she laboriously pulled the big gray bag out of the closet, my excitement grew, as I could hear the tinkling of the bells she had placed at the tie at the top. Sometimes the bag was so full, Grandma had to pull as hard as she could, reminding me very much of the time I watched my grandpa wrangle in what he said was the biggest fish in the lake. She would thrust her little round body forward, brace her skinny little legs, and pull back with all her might. Grandpa had passed away several years before, but often I would see the same mannerisms in my grandma that reminded me of him. If I reached out to help her, I would be stopped by her regular hand wave, signifying, *I've got this! I may be in my sixties, but I'll keep doing it until I can't.*

I would step back and scream with delight as any piece of clothing I ever needed seemed to miraculously appear when Grandma plunged her head and upper body into that old gray army bag. She would reappear with a dress, a warm coat for winter, or a sweater for chilly days. Whatever I needed at the time. They usually would be a little worn or faded, but the perfect size, almost. I tried this later with my own children, but to them it was never magical. Instead, it was just Mom looking for a hand-me-down that they could wear until she could buy them something new. Grandma made it special and always magical.

Grandma went in that bag that morning with vigor, coming out two or three times with that ever-pensive look on her face. She finally went in a third time as if she were going in for the win, flailing her arms as if she were a champion swimmer. Coming up and out the third time, she put her hands on her hips, looked at me, looked at the bag, and looked back at me. For a moment, she had that look on her face I learned to know and love. It meant, *Difficult is hard, but impossible might take a little more time.* "Well, sweetie," she said, "it looks like we're going to have to do something else. The magic bag just isn't doing its job today." Grandma had a plan. She always had a plan, just like she always had a smile on her face.

Grandma never carried a purse. Instead, she would find a little piece of material from the magic bag, very near the color of the dresses she had. She would hand stitch a little pocket just above the right breast of each dress. That little pocket would have a flap that folded down and buttoned. Here she would keep what she called her "go-to" cash. She had a little snap leather purse that would expand depending on how many coins and/or bills she would have in it. This little change purse would fit in that little homemade pocket perfectly. This was something else Grandma kept at bay. Often, when we were shopping, she would turn away and pull out that little purse, making sure there were always enough funds to pay for what was being purchased. I didn't even try to look because I always knew Grandma was in charge and we were safe, which was the complete opposite of what I felt at home.

Afterward, we both pushed the big, gray, magic bag back into the closet—Grandma always let me help. I think by the time she got the bag out, she was ready and willing for a little help in putting it back. She would only let me take it to the door, because I only ever got to feel the cool air coming from that dark but magical closet.

Grandma shooed me off to find our favorite book. My grandma still enjoyed reading to me. Because I wasn't a baby anymore, I would sit very close to her in her big, overstuffed rocker. While leaning against her warm body, I would feel safe and secure as she would read our favorite book. We were reading *Heidi*, and I remember wondering if Heidi could have loved her grandpa any more than I loved my grandma. Later that evening after dinner, Grandma said, "Sweetie, let's sit down and talk."

Something told me this wasn't just a regular talk about the day—this was something very important. After my bath, and having changed into my pajamas, I went back and sat next to Grandma, waiting anxiously for what she was about to say.

"Sweetie," she said, "go get your old shoes."

I retrieved them and returned, handed them to her, and she examined them, letting out a sigh and exclaiming, "Yes! It's time for you to have another pair." She looked at the shoes and looked at me. "Tomorrow," she said, "we are taking the bus uptown, and we are going to buy you some new shoes."

"What?!" I squealed. I had never had a pair of store-bought shoes, and the thought took me by surprise.

Taking the bus uptown was a highlight of coming to Grandma's. We would often take the bus to the park above Main Street to feed the ducks. I loved riding the bus and passing the parks with children playing, people walking dogs, flowers blooming, and green, green grass. I would sit on the side with the window, with the full wind blowing in my face, sometimes catching the breeze with my hand. Once at the last stop at the top of Main Street, we would step out and walk a ways into a beautiful park, where we would take the breadcrumbs Grandma had carefully scraped from the kitchen counter throughout the week and put into a little brown paper bag. Along with the crumbs, Grandma would include the heel of each loaf. We would find a park bench and immediately watch as hungry little ducks would come over for the few crumbs.

Grandma would always say, "Sweetie, these little ducks are coming over because they have never seen such a pretty little girl as you are." This was something I only heard from my grandma, and when I was with her, I believed her. I always felt like I was worthy, loved, and enough.

I thought morning would never come. Grandma knew I was afraid of the dark and had put a pretty pink night-light in the wall socket where I could see it. As I looked at it that night, I imagined being a ballerina gliding across the stage on my tippy toes. In Grandma's garden, visible from the dining room window, was a stone bench. Never in all the years I had been in that garden had I asked where it came from. I always thought it was there especially for me. Grandma would watch from the dining room window as I performed atop that big stone bench. I would sing, dance and dramatically recite "Mary Had a Little Lamb" or other rhymes while Grandma watched from the open window, where she clapped and waved me on for more. The dining room window was quite high, and she looked down on me as if she was cheering from a balcony of a theater. I waved my arms and felt like I was the greatest little performer in the world. Grandma made my world seem special . . . always.

I awoke at the break of dawn, or so it seemed. I could smell the mush cooking in the kitchen. Mush back then was a lot like Cream of Wheat in today's world. Grandma would make it thick because she said it would "stick to my ribs." To this day, I still love thick oatmeal, and I find it very comforting.

"Come eat your breakfast, Sharon," Grandma was yelling from the kitchen. I always wondered why she thought she had to yell so loud when I was just in the next room. I later realized she was losing her hearing.

"Coming," I said, and I was out there in a flash. Today was the day for new shoes.

Grandma always made a little extra mush for the birds and critters. After it cooled, it formed a solid lump the shape of the pot. My job every morning was to take the pot outside by the tree and dump that big piece of mush on the lawn. It would splat on the ground, and I would take the pot and go back in the house. I'm not sure if the birds ate it, but some critter found its way to that big splat because it was gone the next morning.

When I got back to the kitchen, Grandma had taken down the big can of peanut butter and had four big slices of bread sitting on the counter, waiting to be slathered with the thickest peanut butter I would ever experience in my life. To this day, I have never seen peanut butter as thick as was in that big #2 can from the top shelf in Grandma's kitchen cupboard. Grandma's spreading spatula went into that can as she spread a couple of generous layers onto that now three- or four-day-old bread. When the sandwiches were made, they were plopped into a brown paper sack. Grandma then took two five-ounce empty jars out of the cupboard that she kept especially for red punch to take to the park. She poured the punch in carefully, tightened the lids, and deposited them on top of the peanut butter sandwiches in the brown paper sack.

It was a beautiful summer day as we made our way to the bus stop a short distance from the house. Grandma wore her Sunday-best dress and insisted I do the same. Mine was a pretty pink cotton frock. It was sleeveless and a little too short, but perfect for this special occasion. Grandma had retrieved it a couple of weeks before from her mysterious, magical bag.

I never minded that the bus was always late. I loved the anticipation of watching and waiting for it to arrive. As I stepped out a little closer to the curb, straining my neck as I looked up the road, I was taken by surprise to see a big, blue shiny car pull up beside us. I stepped back by Grandma and watched as an elderly lady about her age leaned over and rolled down the window. "Hello, lovelies," she said. "Are you waiting for the bus to go uptown?"

I waited, knowing Grandma would tell the woman with the big blue feather in the oversized hat that yes, we were going uptown, and then she could be on her way. Grandma immediately stepped to the open window as if her very best friend had just pulled up. "We sure are," she replied.

"So am I," the woman said. "Hop in and I'll take you."

My heart sunk. I loved riding the bus. I loved catching the wind in my hand as I looked out the window high up in that big bus. *No,* I thought to myself. I knew

Grandma's first thought was the savings of the bus fare. Forty cents would make a nice addition to the purchase of the new shoes.

When I got in the back seat of that shiny blue car, I sat down to the feel of soft plush and comfort I hadn't experienced before. As the car started down the road, I automatically leaned back and felt comfortable and relaxed. The radio was playing a rendition of Patti Page singing, "(How Much Is) That Doggie in the Window?" Maybe this wasn't such a bad idea after all.

The woman wore the same dark red lipstick as my grandma, her face wore the wrinkles of someone the same age as Grandma, and her big hat jiggled on her head as she immediately started up a conversation. After a couple of minutes, it was as if two old friends had come together after a long separation. I leaned in as they talked, watching and listening. The woman introduced herself as Hazel and said she was going uptown to do some window shopping. I wasn't sure what that was, but it sounded fun and something I would like to do. Grandma told her we were going to buy new shoes, and a sudden smile spread across my face. I leaned back as the women continued to chatter. I held the brown paper sack close to my side and thought how happy the ducks would be to get the breadcrumbs we had saved for them, and how happy I was to think about the purchase of my own brand-new shoes.

Hazel and my grandma each found a piece of paper in their purses to jot down each other's phone numbers, gave each other hugs, and Grandma and I stepped out of the big blue car. It seemed to take a long time for the blue car to finally pull all the way past us. I remember thinking it was the longest car I had ever seen. As Hazel and her car passed by us, I noticed what I could only describe as wings above the back tires. *Wow!* I thought. *I wonder if that car not only played Patti Page on the radio, but maybe it could fly, too.*

As excited as I was to start our hunt for my new shoes, I remember spending a few seconds hoping we would see Hazel again. I pictured myself flying through the sky in the big blue car, with Hazel at the wheel. The thought quickly left my mind. That, I thought, might be a little scary.

Grandma looked to make sure I still had the brown paper sack in my possession and then took my hand. We were at the top of Main Street, where she had asked Hazel to drop us off. "Look, Sharon," she said as she pointed to the mismatch of lined-up buildings on either side of a two-lane road. "That's Main Street." Because the bus driver dropped us off at a completely different location next to the city park, I had never seen Main Street or its buildings before. I stood gazing—the scene was magical. I wondered why Grandma knew so much. Surely she hadn't come without me. That's how important I saw myself in her eyes.

Grandma looked and stood silent. I knew she was surveying the main street and making the plan of what we would do next. Grandma always had a plan, and it always seemed to work out. Maybe not always perfect, but the results were never disappointing.

Not far from where we stood was a little park equipped with park benches and even a pond. I screamed in delight, "Look, Grandma, I see ducks." I wondered if the little creatures could smell the breadcrumbs.

Grandma was too involved in her plan to notice. "OK, sweetie," she said, "we will start down this side of Main Street and visit all the stores. If we don't find your new shoes in any of them on this side"—she waved her right arm up and down as if to make the point even more clear—"we'll come back up to the park, eat our lunches, feed the ducks, and then we will start down this side of the street." With these instructions, she waved her left arm up and down.

She looked at me, making sure I understood. I nodded. It was very important to Grandma that I always understood. Whenever she would explain anything to me, she would look me in the eyes, waiting for a response. I always loved and appreciated this about her. Because I was just a kid, most people in my life would just tell me what was going on and never cared about asking me how I felt. Not Grandma. She always respected my feelings . . . always.

Grandma turned slightly, took out her little bulging change purse from her breast pocket, looked inside, and quickly closed it. Even as a little girl, I knew she didn't have much money. I also knew what she did have, she shared however she could.

I loved the sun beating down on my bare arms. Even though the brown paper bag seemed a little heavy to carry, I was glad to know we had food to eat, which wasn't always the case in my small, unpredictable world.

Unlike the Main Street buildings of today, where many of the buildings are one and the same, these buildings each seemed to have a personality of their own. Different colors, different shapes, and different sizes. Each was a building in and of itself. One thing they all had in common, though, was a display window colorfully coordinated with items of all kinds to draw in the eyes of the beholder. To me, it was a sight to behold indeed.

Entering the first store, Zions Mercantile, I found myself staring up at a well-dressed woman standing completely still atop a platform in the middle of the aisle. Grandma could see my confusion and took the time to explain to me the woman was not real, but rather a mannequin to display the dress that was for sale. The more I saw, the more I came to terms with the world of sales in the big city.

As we walked down the aisles, Grandma would pick up an item or piece of clothing, look at the price tag, roll her eyes, and put it back. We finally came to the aisle with shoes. Grandma looked around, looked at the price tags, and turned slightly to count the money in her little snap purse. "Not here, Sharon, these shoes are not pretty enough for you." At the time, I believed her. Later in my life, I realized Grandma just didn't have enough money to pay for what we saw.

By the time we got to the end of the street, we had gone in every store and Grandma had announced to me that none of the shoes were pretty enough for her beautiful granddaughter. I could have been tired by then, but I absolutely was not. I was more excited than ever to find my brand-new shoes that would be pretty enough for me.

Making our way back up to the small park, we found a bench close to the pond and opened up our brown paper sack. The smell of peanut butter made my mouth water. I had worked up an appetite. Grandma laid out a little kerchief between us, on which she placed each sandwich. Next, she set down the little jars of red punch—Kool-Aid in today's world. Grandma asked a blessing on our little meager meal and both of us began eating our very dry, thick peanut butter sandwiches, washing them down with the punch. I quickly looked for a drinking fountain to wash the thick peanut butter from the roof of my mouth, down into my stomach where it belonged. I loved my grandma, but to this day, I can't eat a dry peanut butter sandwich—a staple along with the mush at my grandma's house. I still find the mush memory comforting, but the peanut butter not so much. I will say, it filled my stomach, and I was always grateful for that.

We took out the sack of the weekly saved breadcrumbs and began feeding the ducks, who had already gathered at the foot of the bench where we were sitting. As we threw out the crumbs, my mind took me back to the mannequins. *I wonder if they have names,* I thought.

"Oh, my goodness, Sharon! How can you drink so much water at one time?" Grandma asked. It was more than I wanted, but that stubborn peanut butter just wouldn't unstick from the roof of my mouth. Maybe I would suggest adding a little honey next time. Grandma told me the bees had to work very hard to produce delicious honey, and we should be careful to preserve it for special occasions. Our neighbor, Mrs. York, had hives and would bring over honey occasionally for us to enjoy.

"OK, sweetie, let's go!" Grandma started down the sidewalk that led to Main Street with the vigor of someone much younger than her. Unfortunately, her little body couldn't quite keep up with her enthusiasm.

Each colorful store on this side of the street presented display windows brimming with the newest fashions, household items, and even toys. The department stores even had moving items in their displays. It was as if time had stopped.

"OK," Grandma said, "let's go in Marshalls and see what they have for you." We walked through the displays, Grandma picking up and putting back items with a roll of her eyes—which I now know meant too expensive. We went in Sears Roebuck, Auerbach's, and Woolworth's.

Before entering the Woolworth store, I stopped to watch a little mechanical dog in the display window, wagging its tail and actually barking. As I stood there, my grandma watched me and started to laugh. "Well," she said, "I think we might need to do a little more window shopping, especially around Christmastime. After all, it's free entertainment." As she took my hand, I strained as long as I could to see that little mechanical dog.

Entering the store, I wondered if this would be the one with the shoes pretty enough for me. Finding the shoe department took time. Grandma felt compelled to stop every once in a while to make sure she rolled her eyes at the price tags.

We left, having two more stores to visit, and even though my adventure had been more fun than I could have imagined, I was wondering if we would find my new shoes. The thought only crossed my mind for a moment. I looked at Grandma, who still wore that expression of determination I had seen so often. This determination became a quality in myself that I thanked my grandma for many times throughout my life.

The alley between these last two stores was wider than the others we had seen on Main Street. We passed by walking hand in hand, but Grandma suddenly stopped short. Curious, I looked up, but didn't see anything unusual—just the beautiful puffy clouds and blue sky. She remained unmoved. I then followed her line of sight, and I saw it too! On the side of the Woolworth's building there was a big sign—white with big, bold black letters spelling out the word "Shoes," a large arrow pointing toward the end of the alleyway. There, tucked way back, was a door; a storefront nestled between the last two stores.

Little did I know I was about to learn a life lesson I would pass on to my children, as well as people throughout the world.

"Look!" Grandma said. "Let's go." We followed the arrow to a storefront with one dusty display window. This window was cloudy, with what looked like feeble attempts to remove some of the film. The display consisted of shoes atop lidded shoeboxes. There were a few artificial flowers placed alongside each box.

Above the one door to the entrance was another big sign, exactly like the one on the side of the building. It took both of us to pull that big glass door open. Once inside, we found ourselves in a narrow walkway. On both sides of the walkway were disheveled shoeboxes of every size piled high above our heads. We looked at each other in disbelief. We had just found shoe heaven!

A plump and pretty middle-aged saleslady in a green apron with arms folded and a stern look on her face appeared in the narrow walkway from somewhere behind the boxes. "Be careful where you walk, you two. We don't want these boxes falling in the aisle. It will take me all day to clean it up!" With this warning, Grandma and I crunched closer together.

I saw it first! As I looked far down the aisle, I saw a table in the middle piled high with something. What was it? I squinted my eyes to get a better look. "Grandma! Look!" Grandma was carefully guarding us from the impending disaster of the shoeboxes. She looked in the direction of my pointed finger.

"What?" she asked. She soon knew the answer as she saw the table piled high with a mountain of shoes!

"Let's go," she yelled. The lady in the green apron appeared from somewhere behind the boxes with a look of obvious authority, ready to protest if any of the boxes were to topple down from the high perches on which they were resting.

I started to run toward the big table, with the woman in the green apron telling me to slow down.

Reaching the middle of the aisle, Grandma and I stood in awe. There were shoes, boots, slippers, sandals, sneakers, moccasins, high heels, mukluks, and loafers in any size and color imaginable. While I stood trying to take it all in, Grandma said something. I thought I heard it, but it took a minute to process. "You can have any pair you want, Sharon. Any pair."

What? Any pair? Grandma didn't even step away to check her change purse. Any pair.

"Yes," she said, "any pair." Then I noticed the sign beside the shoes—"70% off."

She stood back, arms folded and smiling. It was the same smile I saw as she watched me eating day-old bread with honey on top.

Where should I start? I went through the shoes with more enthusiasm than I had at Christmastime, opening Grandma's packages.

The lady in the green apron suddenly appeared as some of the shoes, in my excitement, landed on the floor.

"You need to pick those up," she said authoritatively.

"I will! I promise!" I said. She walked away, knowing she had made her point.

I pushed the pile of shoes to either side as I eagerly looked for the ones that would be pretty enough for me. I suddenly stopped. I had made a tunnel of sorts in the middle of the pile of shoes. As I was looking in, a few dropped to the floor. Again, the lady in the green apron appeared.

"You need to pick up those shoes!" she said.

"I will, I promise, I promise." There in the middle, I saw something glimmer yellow—the only yellow I had seen on the whole table. "Yellow . . . my favorite color," I thought out loud!

"Grandma! Look!"

She bent her little body, looking eagerly into the tunnel I had made in that big pile of footwear. "Pull them out," she said, breathlessly, "pull them out!"

I reached my arm in as far as I could and carefully pulled out the pair of shoes that would be a life-changing experience for me.

I pulled out the most beautiful pair of yellow patent-leather shoes I had ever seen. I looked at them and looked at Grandma! Her face lit up. "Put them on," she said.

The shoes were a shiny, yellow patent-leather with a light brown sole and a strap that fastened to a little white daisy on the other side. I sat on the floor, handling those beautiful yellow shoes with care, taking in the excitement.

Suddenly, my heart sank, and I felt warm tears trickling down my face. I looked up expecting Grandma to see my pain and my disappointment, but instead, she had a smile on her face. Why was she not sad? Why wasn't she sad for me?! I didn't understand.

"Grandma," I said, "they are too big!" They were at least two sizes too big! My toes were nowhere near the end, and my heel didn't touch the back of the shoe.

She looked at me, looked at the shoes, and continued to smile. This was my grandma, who loved me more than anyone in the world. My grandma, who always had a solution to anything. Her solutions weren't always perfect, but I was never disappointed.

"Sweetheart," she said, "we will just stuff newspaper in the toes until you grow into them."

"What?" I thought out loud.

Newspaper.

My tears quickly changed to a smile. The kind of smile you can feel as it spreads into your cheeks.

My grandma was a genius.

And stuff newspapers in the toes we did! Lots and lots of wadded-up pieces of the daily newspaper.

No matter that the shoes looked like boats at the bottom of my skinny little legs. No matter that the layers of bandages didn't keep the slipping up and down of the heels from hurting a little bit. No matter that the newspaper hurt the ends of my toes even with two pair of socks. Those shoes were my favorite of any that I can remember. I believed more than ever when Grandma said anything is possible . . . maybe not perfect, but possible.

Also, I learned that difficult is hard and impossible takes a little more time.

I wore those shoes proudly for several years before I grew out of them.

I finally had the shoes that were pretty enough for me.

Best Friends with Firemen

~

We hadn't been married very long. For a little break, we decided to spend some time with Grandma. Bruce had met her before we were married—of course she was one of the first people I introduced him to when we started getting serious. He knew she was one of my favorite people in the whole world, and she was an amazing, slightly eccentric, beautiful, kind and giving grandma.

We were to stay a night in her house during the month of June. I chose this month because June brought my favorite childhood memories—often snuggled next to her on a cool evening, wrapped in a warm blanket on the rustic log furniture, feeling the gentle breeze coming from the canyon.

I would watch the June bugs hit the screen door and either fall to the ground or fly away, if they were lucky enough to make it.

We would usually sit there without anything said. Instead, we would soak up the love we each felt for the other.

Bruce knew this, and I tried to explain the special relationship I shared with her, but feelings are very often hard to express in words.

Grandma was her own person, determined, grateful, self-confident, and she made friends with everyone.

One time, I remember her needing some plumbing done. She didn't know the plumber who came, but after fifteen minutes of having the work done, she had him at the piano singing hymns with her.

No matter who it was, that person was her friend. My mother and her siblings would be a little concerned at times when she would bring strangers from off the street to have dinner and they would end up staying over.

Well, the night finally arrived for us to spend with Grandma. We got there and were met by a lovely kettle of stew and homemade bread.

We visited for a while, sat on her front porch, and waited for the June bugs. They never came. I realized then that childhood memories weren't something that could always be reenacted. It just wasn't the same when you grew up.

Finally, it was time for bed. We slept downstairs, where it was cool and roomy. Grandma always stayed up very late. I often wondered growing up if she went to bed at all. I'm sure she did. However, this was one of her late nights, as we could hear her footsteps on the floor upstairs. Suddenly, she started pacing, and before we knew it, she was knocking on the bedroom door. Opening it, we were met with the bright beam of a flashlight. Grandma was always calm, and announced the lights weren't working upstairs.

Bruce offered to check the fuse box, but she insisted she would just call someone in the morning. Again he offered, but she was insistent.

I told him it likely needed to be checked anyway, and she would probably just call an electrician. I warned him that he might hear her leading the electrician in hymns. We both laughed.

Grandma was up bright and early, and we could smell the toast and a faint aroma of oatmeal, which as a child, we called mush.

Going upstairs, we both grabbed a bowl and piece of toast. "Grandma," I said, "aren't you eating with us?"

"Oh no, dearie . . ." She always called me dearie. "I'm expecting help any minute for the lights."

Taking a bite of my slightly burnt piece of toast, I walked toward her. Bruce was looking in the dining room cupboard for honey to put on the oatmeal.

As he returned to the kitchen, we both heard the sound of sirens. "It sounds like a fire in the neighborhood," Bruce said, and we both looked at each other.

The sound got louder, and I started to panic a little. "Oh, I hope it's not next door," I said.

Bruce immediately stood up, surveying the situation. It was then I realized Grandma was the only one being calm.

"Grandma, we've got to get out of here. I think something must be on fire."

Just then, the front door flew open and a trail of firemen in full gear appeared, pulling a huge fire hose with them. "Evacuate! Evacuate!" they started yelling.

Grandma approached them, nearly being knocked over. "Is this—" one of them started to ask.

"Yes, this is the place, but dearie, there's no reason to be so upset."

The firemen stopped. I was sure they had never been trained for this kind of encounter. I looked for Bruce. He was standing in a far corner of the kitchen with a horrified look on his face.

"Lady, do you realize you called the fire department?" one of the firemen managed to ask.

"Yes, dear, because I knew you big, strong men would take care of the problem."

Still in shock, the head fireman said, "Just what is the problem, ma'am?"

"Well dear, my lights went out last night. Are you sure you handsome young men wouldn't like to stay for breakfast? You look like you've had a rough morning."

"No thanks, ma'am. Do you know where your fuse box is?"

She led them to the basement.

Bruce came out of his hiding place. "Hey, when you said your grandma was a little eccentric, you weren't kidding! Have they gone?"

"No, of course they haven't. They will probably change the fuse in the box and then sing hymns with Grandma. And Bruce, as far as eccentric? I would like to think of her more as a little unconventional, but she always gets things done. After all, we're all a little different in our own way."

I could tell he was thinking about that.

Grandma's Yellow Cadillac

~

Mornings at my house were never pleasant. My mother had manic depression and couldn't get out of bed despite her best efforts. She would yell instructions from her bedroom, telling me what I needed to do. I would make sure my brothers had breakfast. I would get the baby up, change his diaper, give him a bottle, and take him to my mother, where he would snuggle under the warm covers next to her. I loved that he would be warm, but almost envied not being able to crawl in beside her myself.

It was springtime, so my brothers didn't need to be dressed too warmly. I would tuck their shirts in and comb their hair, and after their breakfast, I'd barely have time to get ready myself.

I washed my face, put on my worn jeans, shoes, and shirt, and heard my little brothers yelling for me to hurry because they could see the bus coming.

I hoped this would be the day my mother would receive a postcard from my grandma. My stepdad checked the phone bill carefully every month and forbid my mother from calling my grandma because it would incur long-distance charges. Other people I knew whose families lived a distance away didn't think twice about keeping in touch by telephone, but my mother was terrified to do it. Each month, we would receive an itemized statement of all the calls coming and going from our house. There was no way my grandma could call or any way my mother would dare call out.

So instead, my grandma would send a postcard. A postcard from Grandma always made my mother happy. The postcards used in the fifties were a three-by-five card with the three-cent postage stamped on one side. Grandma was frugal and filled those cards up with more information than you could ever imagine. When she ran out of room, she would write up the margins of the postcard and both sides.

I often thought every postal worker who handled those cards must have been in awe at the amount of personal information she included on that three-by-five-inch space. I imagined everyone seeing the cards must all know us by our first names and want to find out who this lady was who shared everything but the kitchen sink.

Grandma would tell everything about my mother's sisters, brothers, and the family gossip in general.

Yes, the cards made her happy. Grandma would write once a week, maybe more depending on what was going on in the family. I would know immediately when I got home from school if the card had come. Mom would be out of bed, dressed, taking care of my baby brother, and even have something cooking on the stove. If the card didn't come, she would still be in bed.

Every day I would start all over again, wishing for a card from my grandma. That morning as I left on the bus, holding the hands of my little brothers and assuring them they were going to have the best day ever, I began hoping for a card from Grandma.

As I got home, my mother was standing at the door with a smile on her face. The card had come!

As we entered the house, my little brothers ran to the stove to see what Mom was cooking. With her depression as bad as it was, she did the best she could. She had navy beans and a ham hock cooking. The aroma made my mouth water. It was my favorite dish. I would crush as many saltine crackers as I could manage to mix with a bowl of the beans and stir it all together. To this day, I can still smell those delicious and nutritious beans cooking.

She kissed the little boys and sent them to play in the bedroom we shared. They slept on army-cot bunks, and I had my own single army-bed cot across the small room from them. They loved nighttime because I would tell them stories. Mostly from *Grimms' Fairy Tales,* my favorite. Or I would make up stories of my own to tell them until they had fallen asleep.

"Come here, Sharon," my mom said. "This is about you!"

"About me?" She had sat down in the chair next to our small black-and-white TV with the rabbit ears standing at attention. She read the postcard—Grandma had written about my aunts, and then she came to the exciting part.

Grandma always said, "If I ever get any money, I am going to take care of my family, and then I am going to buy me a big yellow Cadillac." I always wondered  what she would do with a big yellow Cadillac since she didn't drive. When I asked her, she said of course Uncle Leonard would take her wherever she needed to go.

Leonard was my mother's brother and my grandma's right-hand man. He seemed to be there at her beck and call. I knew this because she had always mentioned on her postcards the many things he did for her.

As my mother kept reading, she came to a part on the postcard that was written in all caps, but still hard to make out because the letters were so small.

It read: "I SOLD THE PROPERTY AND HAVE BOUGHT ME A BIG YELLOW CADILLAC."

My mother stopped to see the expression on my face! I didn't realize I could suck so much air into my lungs. I held it for a moment, and then said, "What?" My mother read the line again. I was speechless.

"Wait!" she said, "there is more." I waited in anticipation.

It read: "I am bringing the children clothing, some food, and something for you." Grandma always shared whatever she had. Mother continued to read: "The little boys are too young, and I know you need to be there with them, so I am coming to pick Sharon up for a special surprise."

Again I sucked the air into my lungs and said, "What?" Mother continued: "I will be there this Saturday."

It seemed like Saturday would never come. The day Grandma was supposed to arrive, I helped my mother with the little boys, cleaned up the house, and waited by the window. It had been an especially good day. My mother had gotten up, dressed, and even combed her hair. Grandma coming was a big deal.

My mother braided my long blonde hair and found some hair bows to put at each end of my pigtails. She and I both wondered what the surprise would be.

Grandma would never tell us a specific time she would arrive. She would just write, "Be ready," and ready I was. I sat by the window and waited.

It was a beautiful spring day. Blue sky with big puffy clouds. I was so happy for my grandma that she finally was able to buy her big yellow Cadillac. Grandpa had passed away, leaving Grandma to manage the property they had in southern Utah. No one ever thought it would sell, but it finally did.

Suddenly, I heard the loudest car honk I had ever heard. *Honk! Honk!*

It was Grandma. Mother and I grabbed the little boys and ran outside to meet her. Sure enough, there she was sitting proudly in the back seat of the big, shiny, new yellow Cadillac with Uncle Leonard at the wheel. I soon learned that Grandma preferred the back seat. It didn't restrain her from shouting orders at Uncle Leonard. She definitely was in charge even though he was at the wheel. As I got older, I thought back at what a wonderful man he was to take care of his mother in such a special way.

Grandma got out of the car, "Leonard," she said, "open the trunk." Leonard was a man of little words, but he was always good to Grandma.

Inside were boxes filled with groceries and many, many clothes for each member of the family. Nothing Grandma bought in the way of clothes was ever new. They were hand-me-downs she would acquire from thrift shops and other places. The clothes were often a little faded, but usually the perfect fit, almost.

Leonard carried the boxes in the house. "There's more where this came from," Grandma said. "Don't you worry." My mother got a little teary eyed. "Just don't let that man know or you might have to send everything back."

The little boys went through the boxes with glee while Grandma held each piece of clothing up to them making sure they would fit. Grandma was always fair, but didn't feel it necessary to keep track of what she gave to each member of her family. If it ever came up, I remember Grandma always saying, "I help whoever needs the help the most."

While the little boys were playing with some of the small toys Grandma had brought them, she proceeded to tell my mother and me what the big surprise was. She always wanted me to have as many experiences as I could. Today, I was to go with her and Uncle Leonard on this beautiful spring afternoon to experience something I would never forget in my lifetime.

I grabbed my pink sweater with the pearl buttons Grandma had bought me and we both headed out to the car. Uncle Leonard was at the wheel, looking stoic and very much like the chauffeur of a big, beautiful car.

As I climbed in the back with Grandma, I settled into plush, cushiony blue seats. Frank Sinatra was on the radio singing "When Somebody Loves You" as Grandma reached for her scratchy red-and-white Scottish throw to cover our legs. She patted me gently as she did. I felt very much loved as the touch of her warm hand touched my heart, as well.

Grandma started explaining to me that construction crews had been busy for a couple of years, creating a new road that would give access to more drivers going to the other side of the mountain.

When Grandma explained things, she did it in a way where she never talked down to me. She gave me the benefit of being able to comprehend in adult terms. She always asked me if I understood.

We were on our way to being some of the first to drive through a tunnel that was actually made by digging rock from deep inside the side of the mountain.

I tried to visualize what it was, and it seemed a little bit scary.

The day was beautiful. It was always an adventure being with Grandma. Being in a car instead of riding the bus with her as we always did was a new and fun experience.

As we passed through our town, another town, and another town, the road led us up the hills toward the big, beautiful mountains. The pine trees stood tall and majestic. There wasn't a lot of traffic, and Uncle Leonard paid close attention to the road.

Grandma began pointing out the different shades of green among the pine trees. No matter where we went or what we did, I always learned something new from her.

The big car climbed steadily and smoothly as the road began an incline. I watched ahead as each waving turn in the road brought us closer to the tunnel.

"Look," Grandma said suddenly, "look! There it is." She pointed her finger ahead and squinted her eyes as if she were looking at the tiniest speck of dust imaginable.

I looked, but could see nothing but the road ahead while hearing the whirring of the tires.

"Look, Sharon," she said. "Over there!" At the top of the coming incline, I saw tiny specks and as we followed the curve of the mountain, we got closer, and I realized the specks were cars lined up and slowly moving.

"It's the tunnel," Grandma said.

My heart began to pound in my chest and I moved closer to her. How could I tell her I didn't want to go into that big, dark tunnel? I looked and realized there were no places to turn around. The roaring river was on my side of the car, and the mountain side on the other.

I had to be a good girl, I thought. I trusted Grandma more than anyone else in my life, but this was going to be scary!

The cars were in full sight now, and turning the bend, Uncle Leonard slowed down. "Well," he said, with a little glint in his eye, "this is a sight to behold. Are ya *sure* you want to do this, Sharon?"

"Hush, Leonard," Grandma said. "Of course she does."

Though Uncle Leonard was a man of little words, when he had the chance to tease someone, he always did it.

With that, we found ourselves in the line to enter the tunnel. I looked ahead and saw two cars in front of us. We entered the tunnel and I immediately covered my eyes.

"Sharon," Grandma said. "Open your eyes and look toward the light." I shook my head and kept my eyes covered.

"Sharon," she said softly. "Sharon, open your eyes and look toward the light." She removed my hands gently and pointed my face in the direction of the light.

It was tiny, and hard to see, but it was definitely there. A tiny opening with a light shining through. The car moved slowly, but the light seemed to grow brighter and brighter.

My heart stopped pounding. I sat up and looked toward the light at the end of the tunnel. As we got closer, I realized the tunnel wasn't as long as I thought it would be, and reaching the other end, the light shone brighter and brighter, and I knew it was a perfect day.

At the exit, there was a place for the car to pull off the road. "Leonard," Grandma said, "pull over for a few minutes, would you?"

"Sure, Mom," he said. "How's our little girl doin'?"

"She's fine. We just need to have a little talk, is all."

"Sweetheart," she said as she tipped my chin and spoke to my heart, "in your lifetime, you will experience many dark days. On those days, you will feel like you felt in the tunnel . . . How did you feel?"

"It was dark, and I was scared, and I didn't think I would ever see the light. I know that's dumb," I said, "but that's how I felt."

"Well, that's probably how you will feel many times in your life to come. But how did you feel when you saw the light?"

"My heart stopped pounding," I said. "I was happy, and I knew the light was there and I didn't need to be scared anymore."

Grandma nodded her head and looked me in the eyes with more love than I could ever explain in words. "The thing to remember," she said, "is on those dark days when you don't think there is a light anywhere, remember this: Look for the light. The light will guide you out of the darkness."

"But where *is* my light, Grandma?" I asked.

She put her finger lightly on my heart. "It's here," she said. "We all were given a light. We own it. It belongs to each of us. We just need to bring it forth and it will guide us through the darkest days."

Uncle Leonard had turned so as to hear what Grandma was telling me. This man of little words, stoic and a little hardened, had a tear on his cheek as she concluded, "You begin with faith and hope. You follow it with prayer, and you finally believe, and that light will be there for you . . . to guide you . . . to direct you and to comfort you."

That experience and conversation has stayed with me my entire life. It has reminded me many times of the importance of faith and hope. And it continues to guide me and direct me to this day.

The Waterslide Story

~

*I*f you've ever spent time in Utah in August, you are
aware of the unbearable heat that prompts most people
to find things to do during the day that offer water, shade,
and anything else that creates a cooling atmosphere.

Our family has always been the same. One hot August
afternoon, all of us were sitting around, children and
grandchildren included. After the kids became bored
with the indoor activities, someone, probably one of the
grandchildren, suggested we all hop in the cars and head
to Lava Hot Springs, Idaho. That is where the famous
hot springs bubble up.

The big attraction for the kids was the three-acre
water park, including the four curly tube slides. The
adults looked forward to the cooler Idaho temperature
and the relaxation as they spread out the umbrellas, sat
back in their favorite folding chair with their favorite
books to read, or slathered themselves with tanning
lotion. With that, we would wave the kids off to enjoy
the pool and the amenities.

We all packed in the car, and two hours later had sent the kids to the waterslides and into the pools while the adults lay out or sat in comfy lounge chairs for an afternoon of relaxation.

Donning my earplugs so I could read my favorite book quietly, I looked up occasionally to wave to my brave little grandchildren, yelling for me to watch as they slid down the colorful enclosed twirly slide, laughing and screaming as they appeared out the end. Thinking they all had tried it at least once, I turned to my book and pulled my hat closer over my eyes to relax.

I was brought out of my comfortable trance as I looked up and saw three of my grandchildren standing in front of me with their big, beautiful smiles. "Hey, I saw you," I said. "You were so brave to go down those waterslides."

"Yeah." They all looked at each other in agreement. "But guess what, Grandma?"

"What?" I asked enthusiastically as I looked down to read the rest of the paragraph on the page.

"Guess what?" I looked up. "We want you to go down the waterslide, too."

I was sure I misunderstood. "You mean you want me to watch while you go down again? Sure! Of course I will."

"No, Grandma, we want you to go down the waterslide."

I realized I hadn't misunderstood. "Yeah, I thought that's what you said. Hey, guys, grandmas don't do waterslides."

"We know, Grandma, but we want you to be the first grandma ever! Please, please, come on . . . it will be fun!"

"I absolutely will not go on the waterslide. I'm in my fifties. I'm too old, not brave enough, and will absolutely not do it."

"Grandma, we always thought you were brave!"

A few minutes later, as I stood in line, ready to mount the steps of the yellow curly tube slide, I felt my heart beat almost out of my chest. Looking back, my grandchildren were high-fiving each other and yelling encouragement. "Come on, Grandma! You can do it! Go, Grandma, go, Grandma!"

I honestly think they thought it would be an experience I would continue to thank them for, and something they could brag about to their friends. After all, I probably was the first grandma, other than a first-class middle-aged athlete to go down a yellow curling tube-like structure at anywhere from zero to a hundred with no idea whatsoever of the mental and physical consequences.

I looked back again, opening my mouth to call out for them to save me. But it was too late. I was being gently shoved up the stairs by a tiny little girl who was obviously in a hurry to take her turn. "Is it scary?" I asked.

"Only if you're a crybaby," she said indignantly. With that, she let out a purposely forced sigh of impatience.

Climbing up those narrow stairs definitely not made for a woman my age, I felt the wobble and prayed my weight wouldn't have me crashing to the bottom, taking the line of little kids with me. I was terrified.

Taking a few deep breaths and seeing the grade-school-aged children in front of me, I mustered up the courage to keep climbing. As I reached the top, I saw a tall, skinny boy with large glasses who stood at the railing on the platform. I heard him say, "Next," each time another child disappeared into the ominous round opening.

I didn't dare look at the bottom. It took all of my courage just to focus on the entrance. I stepped on the platform, looking at the boy whose job it was to say *next*. "How do I do this?" I almost pleaded.

He looked at me with the word "Ne—" coming out of his mouth. "Fold your arms."

"Fold my arms?"

"Lady, I'm sorry. I'm just here to make sure you don't fall off the platform and to keep it going. Next!" He looked at me. Out of the corner of his mouth, he said, "I don't know what to tell you. You are the first old person I've seen up here, but you gotta go."

I sat down, closed my eyes tightly, and felt my forehead touch the top of the rim. Down I went, swirling, twirling, banging against the sides, not daring to open my eyes.

Suddenly, I stopped. There had been a malfunction, I knew it! I was lying flat on my back under a mountain of rushing water. I was going to die for sure; I couldn't hold my breath much longer. I didn't dare open my eyes. I was stuck, horrified.

I felt a hand take my arm and pull me up. I gasped, and realized I was at the bottom of the slide and all I had to do was open my eyes and sit up. My son and husband, struggling to hold in their laughter, asked, "Are you OK?"

"Yeah, I'm OK."

They both put their arms around me. "No! Don't do that now," I said, "the kids will see it." I straightened my shoulders and walked away.

"Where are you going, Mom?"

"Back to the waterslide for another ride of my life."

Angels Among Us

The first day of sixth grade at Verdeland Park Elementary brought a big surprise for me and a handful of my other classmates.

When we arrived at school, our teacher told us the class was too full and asked us who wanted to attend Whitesides Elementary instead that year.

Thinking back, I found it very peculiar that our parents were not notified. But that morning a few of us raised our hands and were sent on our way to attend Whitesides Elementary, a significant distance away.

The school was located in an upper-middle-class neighborhood, which was much different from the one we were coming from.

We knew we were different. We dressed different from the kids who wore the latest fashions and just seemed happier than the rest of us.

For the most part, however, they treated us well.

The first thing I noticed were the beautiful shoes the girls in my class were wearing. They were white and looked like sneakers, but were made from a very soft leather. Each girl had different colored laces. I soon learned they were Joyce shoes. My shoes were made from a heavy suede, and had thick soles and a zipper on the side. They were big for me because my parents told me they had to last me throughout the school year and into the next. I hated them. They were heavy on my feet and stood out as being the ugliest shoes in the class.

I found myself wishing for the shoes. The student desks were paired in our classroom, and the girl sitting next to me watched as I couldn't take my eyes off her Joyce shoes with the pink laces.

One day, she leaned over and whispered, "Sharon, do you want to try on my shoes?"

"Can I?"

She was going to actually let me try on her beautiful Joyce shoes.

"Yes," I whispered as Mr. Larsen was energetically drawing stratus and cumulus clouds on the blackboard. She took her shoes off and pushed them over.

"Do you want to try my shoes on?" I asked.

She looked at me with terror. "No," she said, eyeing my big, heavy black shoes. "No. That's okay. You can just try mine on."

I couldn't believe how light they felt on my feet. And I immediately started tapping my toes on the floor.

Mr. Larsen stopped his illustrations, turned around, looked at me, and said, "Sharon! Stop tapping your feet!"

As soon as his head was turned, I couldn't help it. I started tapping my feet with the shoes that felt like I was stepping on those big, billowy clouds he was drawing on the board.

Again, he turned around. "SHARON! STOP TAPPING YOUR FEET!"

My generous friend then said, "Could I have my shoes back now?" I wanted to say, *No, please don't take them back*. I pushed them over to her and put on my black suede shoes with the heavy soles.

Even though I knew there was no way my parents could or would buy them for me, I continued to wish for and want a pair of Joyce shoes.

As the week went by, with Saturday approaching, I looked forward to being able to tend Mrs. Sylvester's three little boys while she went to the market. I loved tending for her. Even though those little boys were all over the place, she always had something special in the fridge just for me. It could be a donut, a piece of cake, or some other treat. When she got back, she would give me a shiny twenty-five-cent piece.

That day as she put the coin in my hands, I suddenly had an idea!

Monday couldn't come soon enough. When I got to school, I asked my friend where she got her shoes. She told me her mother had purchased them for her at JC Penney. Sadly, I realized that could never happen for me.

The next Saturday, as I crossed the street to take care of Mrs. Sylvester's rambunctious and beautiful little boys, ages three, two, and five months, I did it with a smile— even though I had two diapers to change and a little boy who wanted everything that was out of his reach. And even though there were treats in the fridge especially for me, in the back of my mind was the image of me wearing a pair of Joyce shoes all my own.

"Mrs. Sylvester," I said, "do you think I could tend the little boys more for you?"

"I'm sorry, Sharon. It's just not in my budget right now," she said, patting my shoulder.

As I left holding the shiny quarter in my hand, I crossed the street and told my mother I was going to take a walk. I knew it wouldn't do any good if she knew how bad I wanted those shoes. I had to do it myself.

I walked all the way to JC Penney (I finally figured out it was quite a distance for a little girl). I entered the store and was met by the most beautiful kind eyes I had ever seen. A lovely gray-haired woman approached me with a smile that made my heart melt.

"Hello," she said, "what can I help you with?"

"Do you have Joyce shoes that would fit me?"

"I certainly do. Are you here by yourself?"

"Yes," I replied. "How much are they?"

"Well," she said, "they are six fifty. Would you like to try on a pair?"

She smiled and looked me straight in the eyes, with love and what seemed to be a little bit of concern. "Sit here," she said.

She soon appeared from a back room carrying a shoebox, which she laid at my feet. Gently, she removed my embarrassing, ugly suede shoes and expertly placed the Joyce shoes with pink laces on my feet.

"Just your size," she said with a little twinkling laugh. She looked up at me. "If you want different colored laces, I have more to choose from."

"I only have a quarter, but can I put them on Put Away for now?"

"Do you mean Layaway?" she asked.

I had heard Mrs. Sylvester use that term and had asked what it meant.

"Yes," I said, "Layaway." You paid over time, and after you had paid in full, you could take your item home.

"Well," the beautiful woman said, "Layaway usually requires twenty percent down."

We had been learning about percentages in school. I quickly figured it out in my head. "That would be a dollar and thirty cents," I said.

"Yes," she said, smiling again with a concerned look in her eyes.

"I only have twenty-five cents, but I will come every week until they are paid for."

The concern in her eyes deepened. "Okay," she said.

She got the Layaway card. "What is your name, sweetheart?"

"Sharon," I replied.

She wrote my name, the total of the shoes, and deducted twenty-five cents. "There!" she said. "See you next week. You"—she pointed her finger at me—"are a determined little girl."

I left JC Penney with all the confidence in the world that I would be tapping my toes under my desk while wearing my very own shoes with pink laces.

I continued to return to the store and was always greeted by Ellen, the beautiful lady with the eyes that made my heart happy when she looked at me.

I don't remember ever thinking about how many quarters I would need before the shoes were mine. I just remember looking forward to going every Saturday so I could take my quarter to pay on my Layaway and to see Ellen, who soon became my special friend.

One Saturday, as I made my way with my quarter tightly held in my hand, little did I know I would soon be taught a life lesson that would stay with me for decades and become part of my life forever.

Ellen had long since known about the exact time I would be arriving at the store and would meet me at the door. We would walk to the counter, where she would get the box with the names and records of people, who, like me, were coming in and depositing money on an item they really wanted to own. This day was different. Ellen still met me at the door, but took my hand and led me to a sitting area with a sofa for customers. As she sat next to me, her beautiful eyes met mine and I felt a concern and love that I had felt from few people at this point in my life. She looked at me for a long time, and it seemed like my heart would burst from the love I felt from her.

"Sharon," she said, "you are a determined little girl. You have come every Saturday for weeks to put your hard-earned quarter on shoes you have your heart set on.

My accentuated nod confirmed it.

She continued to speak, and the words were coming from deep within her heart. "Even though you have placed a dollar fifty on your Layaway, it is going to take you a long, long time before the balance is complete."

I felt scared that maybe someone else with more money had bought my shoes. I responded, with tears welling up in my eyes, "But Ellen," I said "I will come every week. I will . . ."

She put a soft finger to my lips. "Shhh," she said gently.

I suddenly remembered being held and rocked as a baby, with my grandma soothing me with that same sound. Immediately, I felt comforted.

"I have a surprise for you today," she continued. Her tone changed to excitement, and I felt a huge smile stream across my face.

"A surprise?"

"Yes, a surprise."

She then went back into the storage room where she first brought out the box that contained the shoes I had dreamed of for months. As she approached, I saw the pink laces hanging over the side.

She knelt down and carefully removed the shoes that were deemed the ugliest in the class. No one ever said that to me, but I knew.

As she took the first shoe out, I wondered what was happening. Maybe she thought my feet had grown in a few weeks and she wanted me to have the right size.

After both were placed on my feet, she looked up at me. "These . . ." she said, as she patted my knee. "These are now yours."

I didn't understand; I looked at her, confused.

Before she could speak, I blurted out, "No! I haven't paid for them . . . but I promise I will. I will come every Saturday until they are paid for."

Again, she gently looked me in the eyes, making the "shhh" sound that immediately comforted me.

"These shoes," she said softly, "are my gift to you."

I still didn't understand.

"Sharon," she said, "life is made sweeter for everyone when a gift is given from the heart. I know how much you have wanted these shoes and I am giving them to you. There is no more balance." She showed me the Layaway card, which read, "Paid In Full."

I looked at my shoes, looked at Ellen, and suddenly felt the biggest lump welling up in my throat as the tears started running down my rosy cheeks. "You . . . *you paid for them?*"

"Yes, I did, and it made me so happy to do this for you."

It was real. Ellen had given me a beautiful gift and it wasn't even Christmas, and she wasn't even my grandma.

"Thank you," I managed to say through my tears.

"You are welcome, sweet Sharon. But I have one request." I looked at her, knowing she was an angel; the first of many to come in my life. "I only ask that as you grow up—become more independent—that you watch for opportunities to bless the lives of others. Not only with material things, but also with your heart. You are a special little girl, and you have a lot to offer the world, Sharon. You will understand my words more as you mature."

"I understand," I said. "I want to have a good heart like you."

She rose from the position she was in while placing the shoes on my feet, took my hand, and led me to the door. "Now go," she said, "go my little angel and fly away with those beautiful Joyce shoes . . . And don't forget to come and visit me."

That I did.

Beauty Is More Than Skin Deep

~

My mother looked at my sad face as I came in the house after attending another day of fifth grade. "What's wrong now?" she asked.

"Just the same thing," I said, tossing my fifth-grade reader on the table, nearly knocking over a glass of water she was drinking.

I plopped on the sofa with an obviously dramatic and yet genuinely sad sigh. "I'm just sad because I have these freckles all over my face. I'm tired of being called Freckle Face."

My mother didn't hear me. She had gone out of the room. I wished for once when she asked me a question about myself, she would at least wait to hear the answer.

"Oh well," I said, as I pulled myself from the sofa, changed my clothes, and headed to the kitchen, where my mother had told me to peel the potatoes for dinner.

Fifth-graders, especially the boys, were cruel to the girls they didn't think had a pretty face. As shallow as it seems, this is just the way it was. At least in this fifth-grade class.

Unfortunately, I was a target for bullies.

As the school year went on, every recess I was the object of teasing and rude comments from the mean boys in my class.

One day, I went to my teacher. "The boys keep calling me Freckle Face," I pleaded.

"Just ignore them," she said.

But they were relentless. The more I would run away and cry, the more fun they had.

The school year carried on, and I hated my freckles more and more. One day coming home from school, I threw my reader on the sofa and leaned back with my usual sigh. Sitting next to me was a *Woman's Day* magazine. I picked it up and lazily started flipping through the pages. I stopped short on one page, brought it closer, and read.

An ad on the bottom of the page, with small letters and the outline of a jar with the lid set at the side, caught my eye. As far as I could tell from the illustrations, it looked as if sparkles were exploding out of the top of that jar.

"Try out famous freckle cream. A new way to get rid of those little brown spots. Guaranteed to work."

I felt my mouth gape open as I read the ad again. "Three dollars a jar. Send cash or check with the order form to . . ."

I sat there for a moment, thinking how my world would

change if only I could have a jar of that magically wonderful miracle cream.

I closed my eyes and pictured myself going to school, walking tall and straight past the boys. I saw them all point their fingers and whistle in approval of how Sharon had changed from freckles to the prettiest girl in that fifth-grade class.

Other daydreams were mostly of getting a new puppy who would cuddle up with me, or a new pair of skates, or becoming the champion hopscotch player. This exceeded them all.

I was shook awake by my mother's voice yelling from the kitchen. "What are you doing just lying around? Get in here and fold the clothes—do you think they're going to fold themselves?"

I stopped by the bathroom, keeping the image of freckle-less Sharon as I stared at myself in the mirror. I had to have a jar of that freckle cream.

That evening, I reached under the mattress and pulled out the empty sachet bag that had contained the little dried flowers my grandma had given me for Christmas. I now used it put away the quarters I earned from my babysitting and the Christmas money I had received from Grandma.

I learned at a young age that money was scarce, I could have no expectations, and when I did get money, it was best to save it. Not because my parents taught me by example, but rather the insecurity I felt because of their poor management of household funds.

I closed my door and emptied the sachet bag onto my bed. There were lots of quarters and a few dimes and nickels. Again, I looked at the ad. Three dollars. Send money or check.

I counted out my money and couldn't believe my eyes. I had exactly three dollars and fifty cents. My heart sunk for a moment when I realized there was no way I could send all those coins in an envelope.

My inexperienced mind raced, and the thought came to me: Tomorrow at lunch, I would take my coins and ask the lunch lady to exchange them for dollars.

I put the coins back, and the sachet bag in my lunch sack. The next morning as I got ready for school, my mom yelled from the kitchen, "Come get your sandwich and put it in your lunch sack."

I didn't have the luxury of school lunches, and instead took my own from home. It usually consisted of a dry sandwich with corned-beef slices. I was given a dime to buy a carton of milk. Lots of times, I would save my dime and drink water instead so I could put the dime into my sachet bag with the other coins. It just made me feel safe knowing I had that little bit of change in my possession. I don't know why.

Mrs. Rich, the cashier in the lunchroom, loved me. Often, she would step back into the kitchen and bring me a piece of cake, a peanut butter cookie, or something else the cooks were serving as a sweet treat with lunch. It always brought a smile to my face.

"Here you go, Sharon. I hear those boys chasing you and calling you names," she said once. "I want you to know I think you are the prettiest little girl with freckles

in the whole fifth-grade class." I had to think about that
. . . I couldn't remember another girl who had freckles.

That day, I approached Mrs. Rich, holding my sachet
bag tightly in my jeans pocket. "Mrs. Rich, do you have
dollars in your lunch-money drawer?"

She looked. "Yes, I do," she replied. "Why, are you
going to rob me?" she'd laughed.

"No, no, but I have lots of change. Could I trade you?"

She looked puzzled. "Yes, I guess so."

I dumped the change from the sachet onto the lunch
counter.

"Whoa . . ." she said. "That's a lot of coins." She carefully
counted out the exact amount of three dollars. "Well,
here ya go. Whatever you have planned now is beyond
me. Now shoo—you are going to be late for class."

I stuffed the three dollars into the sachet bag and into
my jeans pocket.

Again, I saw the image of beautiful me transformed
into the prettiest girl in class with no freckles.

When I got home from school, I immediately went
to my room after doing my chores. I told my mom I had
lots of homework to do.

"Go ahead," she said, "Just don't ask me for any help.
I don't get that fifth-grade stuff."

I had found an old envelope in the kitchen drawer
and began to pen the address. I searched and searched
through the clutter in the desk and found two three-
cent stamps. Pasting them on the envelope, I tucked the
piece of paper with my name and address, put the exact

amount in the envelope, and carried it to the mailbox, flipping up the flag. Now I just had to wait.

It seemed like weeks before I heard back. I went to the mailbox every day in spite of the ad reading, "Don't expect the product to arrive for two weeks."

The teasing continued and I continued to react. I just had to have the miracle and everything would change, I thought.

Finally, two weeks and two days after sending the order, I hurried home to find the box addressed to me sitting on top of a few letters in the mailbox. I grabbed it, leaving the rest of the mail behind, knowing my mother would finally collect it. She waited days sometimes before bringing the mail in. It was always an upsetting moment when she did. "Bills, bills, bills," she would say, slamming the mail on the counter. She would then go to her room and lock the door. The only time she seemed happy to receive mail was when she would get a postcard from my grandma.

I stuffed the jar under my shirt, went to my room and hid it under the mattress.

That evening, my mother had a lot for me to do. All I could think about was applying that cream to my face and being instantly transformed into a beautiful princess.

The next morning, I got up early to do my chores. I could hardly concentrate that day at school, and the boys' teasing didn't seem to bother me.

Nighttime came. I went to my room early, telling my mother I had homework to do. After everyone had gone to bed, I reached under my mattress and pulled out the jar. Turning it around in my hands, I looked at the label and then at the directions.

"Apply a small dab sparingly each night to freckles. Continue for thirty days for best results."

I looked in my little round mirror hanging on my wall. "Sparingly?" I said quietly to myself. "For *thirty* days? I don't have thirty days."

My ten-year-old impatient self looked at the calendar on my wall, which pictured a girl cuddling a puppy. I usually looked at it wishing I could have that puppy. Tonight, I looked at it counting out thirty days. "That's a long time," I said.

I washed my face and put on my pajamas. After brushing my teeth, I sat quietly on my bed to read the directions once more. It said for best results, apply for thirty days.

Best results. *The best results,* I thought, *would be to use it all at once. Yes! That what I'll do.*

I slathered the thick white substance on my face, carefully covering all the freckles. "There!" I sighed.

I slept on my back the entire night. Amazingly, the cream stayed in place except for a few smudges.

No one was awake yet. I quietly went to the bathroom, awaiting the results of the miracle cream that was guaranteed to work.

I stared at the outline of my face and carefully removed the cream with a washcloth, dipping it under the faucet and wringing it out each time. Above the bathroom mirror was a light outlet with a single forty-watt bulb.

I looked closer into the mirror. What I saw was not what I expected. It reflected back a face peering closer into the mirror to find the skin behind my freckles much lighter and the freckles standing out like sore thumbs.

I later realized the cream didn't work at all. What I saw were freckles against skin that had been slightly bleached. To me, it was a disaster. I felt the tears streaming down my face as my mother started calling me to come eat my breakfast and get to school.

Get to school . . . How could I go to school? My whole dream had vanished.

That day, the boys weren't interested in teasing me. They had found kickball was more fun and completely ignored me.

No one seemed to notice the disaster on my face that I had seen. My mother had said nothing.

That afternoon at lunch, I went to the table next to the cashier desk where Mrs. Rich sat. After eating my lunch, I decided not to go to recess, and hoped the lunchroom aides wouldn't make me.

"Mrs. Rich," I said, "Can I talk to you for a minute?

"Sure," she said. "What's going on?"

"Look at my face, what do you see?"

"Hmm . . . I see a pretty girl who doesn't realize beauty is more than skin deep."

Suddenly, I felt like even Mrs. Rich didn't understand, and the tears started welling up in my eyes. "What does that mean?" I asked.

"It means, if you just focus on your outward appearance . . . " She stopped, tapping the little spots on my face. "You begin to think people will only love you for your outward appearance."

"But I just spent three dollars on a jar of freckle cream, and it didn't work."

"Oh . . ." she said. "that's what you did with all that money."

I burst out crying, stifling the sobs so no one else would hear.

She leaned over and shielded me with her body, wrapping her arms around me.

"Sharon," she said, "you are a kind and loving girl. I see your kindness shine through. If you will stop focusing on those freckles and instead focus on putting a bright smile on your face . . . " She tipped my face up to hers. "Show me your brightest smile ever." She made a funny face, and I laughed out loud.

"That's better," she said. "Focus on that happy and on that smile. When you are teased, just flash that bright smile and see what happens."

I did. I don't remember exactly what happened after that. I just remember Mrs. Rich's words. Beauty is more than skin deep, she had said, and she told me I had a beautiful smile. I believed her.

The Ice Cream Delusion

~

The fifties were a great time to be a kid. There weren't a lot of cars on the road or many developments. We played outside for hours, never even touching base with our mothers. When they were ready for us to come home, they stood on the front porch, cupped their hands around their mouths, and screamed our names from the top of their lungs. If she had to call again, when we got home, we knew there would be consequences. Sometimes when our parents decided to punish us, they took their time and even waited until the following day before they decided our fate.

Everyone had bicycles except me. My parents finally decided to go get my mother's old bike out of our grandma's garage and try to fix it up for me to ride. It was the best thing ever. An old silver-colored girl's bike, a step-through frame with a basket on the handlebars. I soon learned to ride it and would find myself going as fast as I could down the sidewalk, flying over bumps with ease.

When we had to stay indoors because of bad weather, we occupied ourselves playing checkers and reading comic books, to list just a few activities. Our biggest and best forms of entertainment took place outside, climbing trees in the nearby gully and anything else our young minds could create.

My friends and I would often visit the huge gully, where we would sit atop an old oak tree overlooking a pretty little babbling brook. One day as we were playing in the stream, we looked up to see several huge brown eyes staring directly at us. Never being around cows before, we were terrified and scrambled up that oak tree in record time. We screamed and yelled at them, unsure if they could find a way to get to us. They finally left on their own. We realized then just how late it was getting, and we were scared again thinking of our consequences when we got home.

Unfortunately for us, when we were in the gully, we really couldn't hear our mothers yelling for us. When we got home from the cow scare, we were in big trouble.

That evening coming home from the gully, we were wet, dirty, tired, and in trouble. It was my stepdad who had brought home ice cream that night. My favorite kind, Neapolitan—strawberry, chocolate, and vanilla layers all in one quart box. When I found out we had it, I went outside, yelling to all my friends, "Hey, everyone, we've got ice cream tonight!" Ice cream was a treat that was few and far between in our neighborhood. If someone's parents had brought ice cream home, every kid in the neighborhood knew about it.

As we finished a supper of corned beef and gravy on bread, my stepdad took out the ice cream. He saw my face light up. He told me I wouldn't be getting any of it. It was my punishment for not coming home on time.

As my family finished with the usual "yums"—you hear when someone is eating something really good— he put the rest in the refrigerator freezer compartment, which was only big enough to hold a quart-sized container. As he put it in, I wondered how much was left.

The next day, Saturday, my parents told me they were going in the car for awhile and I was to stay home. My thoughts immediately went to the fridge freezer, which held the unknown amount of Neapolitan ice cream, left from the night before.

I took out my checker game and began playing both sides by myself. When that got boring, I got out my *Little Lulu* and *Super-Mystery* comic books. Both were worn from many hours of reading them over and over again. I never got tired of reading comics and would trade them with my friends. None of us had very many, but we enjoyed trading them when we had the chance.

My mind kept going back to the ice cream. My parents said they wouldn't be back for an hour and a half. I looked at the clock. They had been gone about thirty minutes, which left me an hour to get up the nerve to see how much of that coveted ice cream was left over.

I finally got up the courage, went to the fridge, took out the quart container, and carefully opened it up. There was nearly a half quart left over. My mouth watered as I looked and then quickly put it back. Again I went to my comics, and again I went to the freezer, taking out the container. This time, however, I had a spoon in my hand.

No, I thought. *A butter knife would be better.* I went to the drawer, got the butter knife, and carefully slid it across the top of the frozen delight. I did it again and again, not realizing how much I was eating. It didn't look like a spoon had been dipped in, but it was noticeably less than when I started. I carefully placed the lid over the rest and waited.

My stepdad always got the last of it, and made it known no one else could. When my parents got home, everything went on as usual. I asked my mother if there was anything I could do for her and went out and cleaned up the yard without even being asked. No one ever noticed when I did it. They just noticed when I didn't.

Suddenly, I heard my stepdad's booming voice coming from inside the house. "Sharon! Come in here."

"Oh no," I thought, "the ice cream!" Sure enough, when I got in, he had the box out and was glaring at me.

"You ate the ice cream."

"Yeah," I said. I waited and waited and waited some more for my punishment. Afraid to ask, I went to bed.

The next morning, my stepdad got me up before he went to work. "I have your punishment."

I just looked at him, not knowing what to say. He looked back. "So you really like ice cream, dontcha?"

Was this a trick question? Did he really ask me if I liked ice cream? I nodded my head in agreement.

"Well," he said, "I have a surprise for you." He didn't say it in a tone of a good surprise. I wondered the whole day what would be in store for me when I got home from school.

My stepdad usually got home from work about the same time I did. It was never pleasant, so I tried to stay out of his way. This evening, I wasn't so lucky. He walked in the house holding a brown sack. He motioned for me to walk over to him with his usual jerk of his head, which meant, *Get over here right now.* I walked over and stood in front of him, expressionless.

"So, you really like ice cream, yeah?"

I didn't know if it was a question I should answer or if I should just nod my head in agreement. "Yeah," I said, "I really like ice cream."

"Well," he said, motioning me to the kitchen table, "*that* is about to come to an end."

What? I almost said it out loud. I had been playing with my friends outside, and they had all gathered on our front steps. It was a hot summer day, and the flies were banging against the screen door.

Usually when the kids were on our steps, he would yell with a wave of his hand, "Get outa here, ya little brats." This time, he said, "Sure, come closer to the screen door so you can see your friend end up with the biggest bellyache, ever."

What? I thought again. He motioned for me to take a seat at the kitchen table, with the kids at the screen door by my side, looking in at what was about to take place.

He took a quart-sized container out of the paper sack. Ice cream! It was ice cream. He opened it. The sides had begun to melt, making a rainbow of strawberry, vanilla, and chocolate ice cream running all together. He handed me a spoon from the kitchen drawer and yelled, "Eat!"

I didn't know whether to yell "thank you" or not. Then I realized that what I was about to do was meant to be a punishment. I took the spoon and started on the melted part of the ice cream. I could hear the gasps coming from my friends.

"Let this be a lesson to all of ya," my stepdad said. He stood by, arms folded, watching me. I quickly caught on. He was making me eat all this ice cream, thinking it would give me a tummy ache. I played into his plan.

"Oh no," I said, after finishing about a third of the quart. "Do I have to eat the rest?" I looked up at him with the most painful look I could muster up.

"Every bit of it," he said. I looked over at my friends and smiled with a sheer look of delight on my face.

One brave little boy by the name of Danny spoke up. "Hey, mister, can I help Sharon with her punishment?"

My stepdad did not respond, but kept standing in back of me with his arms folded, tapping his toe on the floor, quite certain I was going to be writhing in pain with the worst stomachache ever!

When he walked away for a minute, the kids gathered closer to the screen. "How is it, Sharon?"

I looked around. "Great and yummy," I said.

"Do you have a tummy ache?"

"Nope," I whispered. I answered him with the biggest smile he had probably ever seen on my face.

When my stepdad came back, I moaned and groaned and put on the best act I possibly could, making him believe this was the worst punishment ever. When I took the last spoonful, I wiped my finger across the bottom of the box, making sure not to leave any behind.

I looked at my friends out of the corner of my eye and gave them a sly smile. "Can I go to bed now?" I asked my stepdad.

"Your tummy aches, yeah?" he asked.

"Yeah, my tummy aches," I replied.

Truth was, I got out of doing my dishes, went to bed, and read my comics under my covers before I fell asleep, happy and content.

Of course, I let out a moan now and then to make sure my stepdad knew I had had the worst punishment possible for an ice cream snatcher.

The next time we had ice cream, my stepdad said, "I bet you don't want any, right, Sharon?"

Looking at him with the most mournful face imaginable, I said, "Well, maybe just a little bit is all."

"Oh," he said, "you still haven't learned your lesson. With that, he scooped up a huge bowl and handed it to me. I knew the drill.

"Do I have to eat this? All of it?" I asked.

"Every bit," he said.

That was the first and only time I ever put something over on that mean stepdad, and Neapolitan ice cream is still my favorite to this very day.

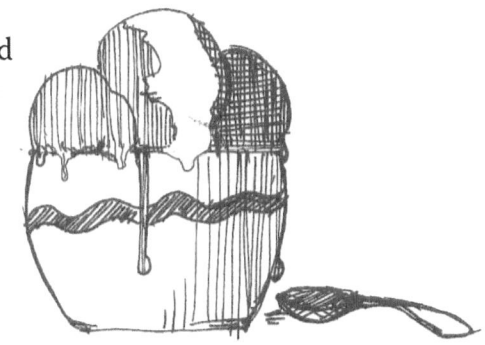

Watch Where You're Shopping!

~

I was very busy when my children were small. I made bread in round cans, baked cakes from scratch, canned everything from deer meat to beets, and made shirts for my husband.

We had a small market in town where everyone did their shopping, mostly on Saturdays. It wasn't a very big market, and when there were bargains, they were usually put in a shopping cart and displayed somewhere at the front of the store. I loved the bargains, and I loved shopping day. I would put on a dress, fix my hair, and apply a little bit of makeup. For me, shopping was a way to spend time by myself. I loved finding the bargains, as well as going up and down the aisles, stopping now and again to talk to a neighbor or two.

One Saturday while shopping, I learned a few valuable life lessons.

As I walked up and down the aisles, picking up miscellaneous items, I noticed at the top of one of the aisles a shopping cart turned sideways in the main walkway.

It was filled to the brim with all different grocery items. I made my way to the cart, excited to be the first one to choose from the array of different items being displayed. I stopped at the front of the coveted bargain cart and started throwing items into my basket. *What a find*, I thought. *I'll just take it all and then decide what I want to keep. Then I'll put the rest back in the cart.*

I was amazed at the variety. Candy corn to bananas, green beans to ground round. Halfway through the cart, I was so focused that I almost missed the foot tapping near the wheel on the other side of the bargain cart.

I slowly looked up to see a tall woman glaring down at me. "That," she said, "is my cart!"

"Sorry . . . I thought it was a barg—"

"I'll do it!" She grabbed the package of sweet rolls from out of my hand as I moved to put it back.

I started to tiptoe away, only to have a firm hand take hold of my shoulder. "Not so fast. You aren't going anywhere until I get this cart unloaded. Of all the nerve," she blurted out. With that, all eyes in the store were upon me. Seeing everyone looking at me, she continued in a very loud voice, "This woman was taking groceries from MY cart!"

I lowered my head. I imagined everyone staring at me even though I couldn't be sure if anyone was continuing to pay attention.

When she had taken out the last stolen item, she walked away indignantly to the nearest checkout, still muttering under her breath.

I walked out of the store, got in my car, and drove home. Needless to say, I returned the same day. After all, we still needed groceries.

The lessons I learned were these: Not all that glitters is gold . . . and watch where you are shopping.

Alice

Sometimes a City Girl and a Cowboy don't find common ground, at first. That is, unless the cowboy has someone or something in their life by the name of Alice . . . which was the case with me and my cowboy.

He was OK, for the most part. Handsome, kind, hardworking, caring, from a lovely family. However, all those things came secondary . . . only to Alice.

Alice was beautiful, with big black eyes and long lashes. Her thick black mane was fun to brush, and she was always ready to go for a ride.

Alice was Bruce's horse. A lovely Black that diverted attention everywhere. She was said to be one of the best-trained horses in the small town where we lived.

I fell in love with Alice immediately.

Having never ridden a horse, I was content to ride with Bruce . . . for the time being.

After we married, however, my tune changed. We moved to his little farming community, where most everyone who were our age had married, and both husband and wife knew how to ride . . . except me.

Every time we would go riding, all the other wives would have their own horses. They knew all about them and were very good riders.

Over and over again, I would ask Bruce to teach me to ride on my own.

"Well," he'd say, "not quite yet. We only have Alice, and you can ride with me."

My argument was that maybe I would like to take Alice by myself or ride her along with the wives—who, I would emphasize, had their *own* horses.

After months of begging, nothing changed.

It was then I decided to take the matter into my own hands. One day after Bruce had gone to work, I put my cowboy (girl) boots on, donned my cowboy (girl) hat, Levi's, and a leather jacket, and headed out to the stable where Alice lived in her spare time. I called her over to the side of the fence and she came immediately. Alice and I were friends, and I was positive she would cooperate with my plan. Next to the stable was the tack room with the big, heavy saddle hanging from a hook on the wall. Next to that were the bit and all other equipment it took to mount up.

I wasn't very big, and trying to get that saddle from off the hook was just not going to work.

Back then, not having the convenience of cell phones, I went into the house and called Pat, the strongest and most capable young wife I knew.

Pat, the only girl raised with a family of five brothers . . . she could do everything. I knew for certain she would be able to at least lift the saddle off the wall and help me with the other parts of carrying out my plan.

So, I called her on the phone.

"Hey, Pat, whaterya up to?"

"Not much," she said, "how about you?"

"Well, I need your help."

"OK, what's going on?"

"Pat, I need you to come help me saddle up Alice."

"Saddle up Alice? Isn't Bruce working?"

Bruce was employed part time at the local furniture store in our little town. It was an up-and-coming little store and employed nearly all the young men in our community either on a part-time or full-time basis. Bruce worked part time while being enrolled in school.

"Yes, he's working."

"Then how are ya goin' to ride Alice? You didn't learn over the weekend, I know that."

"No, I didn't, but I've been taking notes from you and the other wives and I think I can do it . . ."

"Sharon," she said, slowly and deliberately, "are you SURE?"

"Yes, I'm sure."

"Well, OK, then . . . I guess. What do ya want me to do?"

"I want you to come help me lift the saddle off the hook."

"Sharon, that saddle weighs more than you do. Wait . . . you mean you want ME to lift it off the hook and you want ME to put it on Alice?"

"Well, maybe . . ."

"OK, I'll be there in fifteen minutes."

The last thing I wanted Pat to think was that I didn't know how to do anything.

I took stock of Alice's bit and went over in my mind how to fit it to her, along with the reins.

Yes! I thought, *I can do this.*

When Pat got there, she was dressed in her waders and said she had been out in the field helping her brothers take the water. Everyone in that town who owned property had what were called "water shares." Each share entitled the owner to a certain amount of time to draw from the ditch to water their property.

I met her at the truck, and we walked together to the stable and tack room

"Are you sure?" she asked.

"Yes, I'm sure."

"Where are you going?"

"I'm just going to ride in front of the store and let Bruce see that I know what I'm doing."

The store had two big picture windows in front, and that was where the displays went and where Bruce would most often be seen along with the other store personnel, who were grateful to be looking out of those windows while working.

"But you DO know what you are doing?" Pat asked, looking at me out of the corner of her eye.

I didn't answer, but just walked ahead of her, holding my head high in confidence. I just looked at her and let out an indignant sigh.

"OK," she said, "let's do it."

Pat stood about five nine. She was sturdy, strong, and had a captivating persona and smile. Everyone loved her. If she didn't like you, she had no qualms in letting you know it. She liked me. Otherwise, I could have never gotten her to take part in my horse-riding project.

She went to the wall, lifted the saddle off as if it weighed a few pounds, mounted it on Alice, and looked at me. "Do you know how to put her bit in?" she asked.

"Of course I do." And with that, I did it.

Just then, Pat looked at her watch. "Hey, I gotta go. I told Mom I would fix lunch for the boys and I'm gonna be late." With that, she took off for the truck.

"Well, Alice," I said, "it's just you and me."

It was then I discovered the cinch at the underbelly. I reached down, and with all my might, tightened it. Getting a stool from the shed, I brought it over and mounted Alice.

"OK, girl, ya gotta cooperate." I stood there, remembering. To turn left, pull the reins right. To turn right, pull the reins left. Pull back to stop. A little jab at the side to go.

"Got it!" I said out loud.

The store was about a mile up the road, and I knew I could do this.

I reached the end of the driveway—so far, so good. I stood there for a minute, imagining the proud look on Bruce's face when he and his friends would look out the window and see me adeptly riding by myself for the first time.

I imagined what I would look like. Back straight . . . reins in hand . . . Alice completely and positively following the directions of my excellent horse handling.

I smiled. He would be so proud, and I would be so proud of me.

With that, Alice lunged forward.

"Woah, girl. None of that," I whispered gently

I could feel my heart start to race. "Nothing to be afraid of," I said out loud.

Nearing the store, I started to beam. It was one of those smiles you just can't stop from happening.

Just as we got to the window, Alice lunged slightly. With a quick glance, I saw the entire store staff standing at the window. I fell off her, followed by the saddle nearly on top of me.

What just happened? The cinch! I didn't have the cinch tight enough.

Bruce ran out, followed by what seemed to be half the town.

"Sharon! Are you OK?"

I just looked up in utter embarrassment. I saw a few people hiding their faces to keep from showing an outward laugh; others were truly empathetic and concerned about my safety.

Bruce helped me up, gave me a hug, and whispered, "I don't think you cinched her up tight enough."

"DUH!" I said indignantly.

Alice was a good horse. She stood in place through it all.

Bruce walked over, took hold of the reins, and gave me a hand back on Alice.

"Is it all right if I take you and Alice home?" he asked.

"Well, it'll probably be safer," I said.

On the ride home, he promised he would teach me how to ride Alice.

I was never a good rider, but I knew from then on to check to make sure the saddle wasn't going to come off again with me on it.

The Doughnut Story

~

Getting to know people wasn't an easy thing for me, especially with five young children under foot and a husband who worked long hours.

I had a next-door neighbor I dearly loved. I only saw her when she would be out back watering her lawn, but when I got a glimpse of her, I would try to get out there for even a brief conversation. She was older and wiser than me, and always seemed to make me feel better on a busy, and sometimes lonely, day.

I was always surrounded by children, but I lacked social interaction with people more my own age. I thought about it often, but being the somewhat introverted person I was, I lacked the confidence to know how to take the initiative to meet any of my neighbors.

One day, after thinking about it I came up with a plan. *It might work,* I thought to myself as I took out the last batch of laundry from the dryer and set it in disarray on the sofa. The kids were watching *Mr. Rogers* on TV with their dad, so I knew they would be fine while I ran next door for a few minutes.

I grabbed the box of fresh bakery doughnuts from the shelf, along with a can of hot chocolate mix. It was a chilly fall afternoon as I put on my jacket and ran next door, where Shirley was vigorously raking leaves. "Hey, Shirley," I said, almost dropping the doughnuts in a mud puddle as I tried to wave her over.

"Hey," she said. "What's going on Sharon, are you going to a party with all that good stuff you're carrying?"

"I wish," I said. "No, I'm not, but I'm wondering if you know of anyone in the neighborhood my age . . ."

She stopped me. "Of course I do. I've been telling you that you've got to get out there and meet people."

"No, Shirley, wait, let me tell you."

"OK," she said, as she dropped the rake, folded her arms, and gave me her full attention.

"Well, I've been thinking, it's a cold fall day, and everyone loves fresh doughnuts and hot chocolate."

She nodded her head in agreement.

"So, I thought maybe you might know a family in the neighborhood about the same age as mine . . . maybe somebody with colds or something."

"With colds? This time of year, everybody's got colds," she replied, laughing.

"Yeah, I know. But maybe a mom who is home with her sick kids. I could take the doughnuts and a can of hot chocolate and maybe make a friend."

"Sharon, you don't need that to make a friend, but that's a great idea." She stopped, obviously thinking. "Come here," she said.

"Where?" I asked, looking around.

"Over here, where I can point something out to you." She wrapped her arm around my shoulder and brought her head next to mine. Squinting, she pointed. "See that house in back of the one we are looking at?"

"You mean the one across the field and across the road?" I looked in the way of her pointed finger. "Yeah, you mean that one?" I put my hand next to hers and pointed in the same direction.

"Yeah, that one," she said. "That young woman is your age and has three little ones home with colds."

I started off across the street, knowing I would be a visitor with a pleasant surprise that would just make her day. If the kids were too sick, she could enjoy the hot chocolate and as many doughnuts as she wanted. I imagined her sitting on her sofa late that night watching an episode of *The Donna Reed Show*, doughnut in one hand and hot chocolate in the other. All the time thinking of me, her new friend. I was full of excitement.

Crossing the road and walking through someone's unfenced yard, I reached my destination. I was numb with the cold, but warm inside knowing I was just about to make some poor homebound mother's day. It wasn't often I got to feel like a hero. Who would imagine I could do it with doughnuts and hot chocolate?

Setting the can of hot chocolate on the porch and balancing the doughnuts in my other hand, I reached for the doorbell. The sound I heard was unlike any doorbell

I had ever heard. It was like a sudden thud, and then it stopped. In fact, I wasn't sure it was a sound coming from the doorbell at all. I pushed the button again, only to hear the same sound. *Yep, how strange is that?* I thought. *It's the doorbell.*

Maybe I should knock, I decided. *I hope I'm not waking anybody.* I couldn't imagine a mother of three being asleep at three in the afternoon.

Immediately after my soft knock, the door swung open, and I was met with a very tall, stooped-over man with a bald head and beady eyes staring a hole through me. I immediately imagined what it was probably like in a criminal lineup.

"I . . . I . . . I brought you some doughnuts and hot chocolate. It's very cold and everybody loves doughnuts. The hot chocolate is very good. I think your kids will like it . . ." Back then, I had a tendency to talk very fast and run sentences together when I was nervous—and I couldn't remember being this nervous, ever.

He cut me short. "I don't have kids, I don't like hot chocolate, and doughnuts give me diarrhea."

"Uh, yeah, well, I don't know what to say."

"How about you say nothing, and I shut the door." That's exactly what he did.

I didn't know whether to cry or to laugh. I just wasn't sure of the emotion I should have had at that point.

I picked up the chocolate from the porch and headed back. I looked for Shirley, who was just hopping out of her car with an armful of groceries. She took one look at my forlorn face and said, "Just a sec while I take these groceries in the house." She came back to see the tears streaming down my face.

"Oh, sweetie," she said, "what happened?" It was as if she knew immediately. "Oh no, you went to the wrong house, didn't you?"

I nodded. "I guess so."

"Well, look, this time I'll go with you. That person doesn't like people very well."

"Yeah, I noticed."

With that, we headed back to the right house and delivered the doughnuts and hot chocolate mix. We were greeted with happy faces upon seeing the treats.

That night, I imagined my new friend sitting on her sofa, doughnut in one hand, hot chocolate in the other, enjoying the latest episode of *The Donna Reed Show*.

I had a smile on my face and a happy heart.

The Bubble Story

~

I have a surprise for you," he said. "We are going on a little trip." I waited.

He continued, "I worked extra hours this payday to take you on a little vacation."

"Where?" l said. I looked at him in bewilderment.

"To the big city."

I knew the closest city was at least forty miles away. "What on earth are we going to do there?" I asked, thinking he for sure had lost his mind.

He went on. "Our anniversary is coming up. I was doing some checking, and we are going to the Crystal Inn."

He watched my face . . . I was speechless.

"The Crystal Inn," he said, "has a Jacuzzi in the honeymoon suite."

Again, I tried to process.

Seeing the confused look on my face, he repeated, "A Jacuzzi. You know, a Jacuzzi—a king and queen version of a bathtub, but with a whole lot of other stuff." He looked at me, puzzled. "Sharon, we're in the seventies . . . everybody knows what a Jacuzzi is."

"Well, I don't," I said, a little bit offended. "Bruce, it's not like I sit in a Jacuzzi eating bonbons all day . . ."

He pulled out a crumpled, folded-up piece of paper from his Levi's pocket and handed it to me. Sure enough, the advertisement featured a bright pink Jacuzzi with the words, "Come experience the newest addition to our honeymoon suite."

"You mean you made reservations?"

"I sure did," he said. "We are going this Friday. I took a half day off work. We'll eat dinner before we go, stop for a few snacks, and be on our way."

I kept looking at that ostentatious pink Jacuzzi, thinking I was going to do something completely new and different. I felt the excitement build for the new adventure, and looked back at him with the biggest smile, then gave him a hug.

"What time are we coming back home?" I said, wondering if it was an adventure like going swimming or something.

I looked at the picture again. The Jacuzzi stood suspended in air, with steps leading up to it. "Wow, this is pretty fancy," I said, almost to myself.

"We'll stop for breakfast. With gas and everything, I managed to save enough for us to have a nice breakfast at Denny's."

"Whoa," I said, "this is a big deal."

Friday arrived. I scurried to get the kids ready for their overnighter at Grandma's. We didn't usually leave them, and there was an abundance of energetic excitement that filled our house.

We dropped them off and made our way in our yellow Volkswagen Bug.

Almost thirty minutes later, we drove along Highway 89, where colorful fruit stands graced one side of the road, while the majestic rock cliffs of the Wasatch Mountain front were on the other.

We spotted a small mercantile store and decided to stop for a few treats that would hold us over until the much-awaited Denny's breakfast to top off our adventure.

We both grabbed a hand basket and went our separate ways down the narrow aisles of that little country store.

I picked up a copy of *National Enquirer* to catch up on celebrity news, which I knew almost nothing about.

After picking up a bag of chips, something caught my eye on the middle shelf of the next aisle, labeled "Toiletries and Other Stuff." A bright pink bottle featuring bubbles on the label. "BIG BUBBLES" was written in bright blue caps right in the middle.

I could picture the most luxurious, relaxing, carefree bubble bath ever. Concealing the bottle, I headed to the small checkout counter, where a plump middle-aged woman with rosy cheeks and a beautiful smile greeted me.

"Hey, sweetie," she said, "your husband just checked out."

Whew, I thought as I pulled the bubble container from my hiding place. I wanted this part of the adventure to be a surprise.

The woman took a look at my *National Enquirer* as if to get a peek and continued to check me out.

Getting to our destination didn't take long. The next job was to find the Crystal Inn.

It was hard to spot. We were looking for a beautiful structure bedecked with surrounding flowers and a beautiful neon sign suspended from a pole high in the air. I pictured it being brightly lit, with our own personal invitation on the placard—"Welcome, Bruce and Sharon." After all, we were celebrating our anniversary. When I think back at how very naive I was at that age, it scares me.

Well, we were greeted with a neon sign high in the sky, all right, and it was lit up—part of it. The C flickered and the R was completely gone. The rest of the letters were blinking furiously. It gave me a headache, so I stopped looking. I looked back to see if the sign was really tipping to one side. I quickly erased that thought from my mind, knowing we had to enter the check-in door just below it.

"Well, we're here," Bruce said, trying to act and sound enthusiastic. He raised his hand in the gesture of a maître d' ushering us to a table in a fancy restaurant.

I wasn't buying it. We pulled into the parking lot while I wondered how on earth there could be so many empty beer cans in one area and stopped the car under the narrow awning. We walked through the door, which might have read Enter at one time. I wondered if I really wanted to make this commitment or if I wanted to skip the hot-tub adventure and return home safely. I looked at Bruce's face, which appeared as if he had read my thoughts. He gave me a nod and a puppy-eyed expression that read, *Come on . . . let's do this.*

As we entered the office/residence of the Crystal Inn, a woman in an obviously well-worn apron approached us, leaving her half-eaten tuna sandwich on the end table. A heavyset shirtless man lay lazily on a sofa next to it, his bare feet hanging over the arm. He was watching wrestling and was obviously very into it as he shouted out obscenities to what I assumed was the referee.

The woman wiped her hands and her mouth on the café-style apron that could have been white—I really couldn't tell for sure. I knew her sandwich was tuna—I could smell it.

"Are you the out-of-towners?" she asked, as if we were committing a crime.

Bruce lightened up immediately. "Sure are. We've got the honeymoon suite with the Jacuzzi reserved for tonight."

"Ya, I know," she said, handing us the keys anxiously as she looked back at her sandwich, as if making sure someone wasn't going to take it. "Around the back to the west—Room A-1."

Well, maybe that's a sign, I thought. A-1 was the first positive so far.

We drove around the side of the one-level structure. There on the very end was A-1. The blacktop parking lot extended out about thirty feet and ended, meeting a stark gray field of what might have been weeds at one time, but they had all died.

I got out of the car and stood there looking at the door covered in gang-related graffiti, which would lead us to our new hot-tub experience and an evening of much-needed relaxation.

As Bruce opened the door, we were met with a noise that nearly caused both of us to lose our balance as we stumbled backward, wondering how we got in the path of a freight train.

Getting our wits about us, we both looked around at the same time, searching for the tracks with the train that was about to mow us down. Nope, no train. It was coming from within the room. We cautiously entered, having no idea what to expect. Looking around, we realized it was coming from the bathroom. The door was shut.

"Don't go in there," I screamed. Too late. He opened the door. I ducked for cover.

Suddenly, the noise stopped. "Oh," he said. "I think it's the fan. When the door is shut, the fan goes on."

"Well, turn the thing off," I yelled.

"I can't. There's no switch." He opened the door. No noise. He closed the door. The room seemed to vibrate with the sound that emulated a full-blown train-track experience.

I went in to look and was greeted by a small basin, a smaller commode, and a towel rack, on which hung two average-looking motel towels that surprisingly looked normal and clean. Next to the sink was a soap dispenser. I checked to see if it worked. It did. In the corner was a shower. I backed out of the bathroom and turned around to see a full bed with a sunk-in mattress. On the wall facing the bed was a fourteen-inch TV and rabbit ears. Over the TV hung a picture of someone obviously trying to copy Picasso. It didn't work.

To draw my attention away from the room—I was sure of it—Bruce said, "I'm exhausted. I'm going to jump in the shower and change. Why don't you bring this stuff in and check out the Jacuzzi?"

He pointed to the other side of the room. With all the stuff going on and what I was sure was a collision with a freight train, I had neglected to notice the main reason we had come here—the Jacuzzi.

Bruce had closed the door to the bathroom. I looked around and found the room surprisingly clean for a motel. The small end tables at the sides of the bed were adorned with fake pink roses. I pulled down the pink-and-blue bedspread, viewing the sheets, which smelled clean and fresh. I let out a sigh of relief.

Then my eyes met the Jacuzzi. It was a bright pink color, with three overelaborate steps leading up to it. Much smaller than the pink heart-shaped Jacuzzi pictured in the ad.

Bruce had planned this trip for me, and regardless of how everything had turned out at this point, I hoped it would be a memorable evening.

I grabbed the small suitcase, the stacks of treats, the *National Enquirer*, and the small sack that held the bubble bath. At least I could relax in a warm-watered hot tub with a few bubbles without kids pounding on the bathroom door. I felt better already. I wanted to have everything ready by the time Bruce got out of the shower, so I knew I had to step it up.

I laid the overnight bag on the bed and went to the steps with my bubble bottle in hand. The tub was surprisingly clean, except for a few unworthy bugs that had met their doom on the bottom. Taking some tissue, I wiped the bugs up and looked for the knobs to turn on the water, making sure I had the right temp—a little hotter so I could get ready to sink in. I remembered my *National Enquirer* and grabbed it from the bed while the water was running.

I sat on the side of the tub, waiting for it to fill to my desired amount. I couldn't remember the last time I spent my time in just a regular tub.

I took the bottle of bubbles and poured in a generous amount. The side read "36 ounces." I poured the whole bottle in. Why not? I wanted the bubbles to last a long time.

Then I noticed the silver buttons on the side of the Jacuzzi. *Oh, of course,* I thought. Bruce did mention the circulating water. That would be just like a massage.

With him still in the bathroom with the freight-train fan, I pushed the button. Seeing additional buttons, I pushed those and was met with the spontaneous, silent explosion of bubbles extending to the ceiling and over the side of the pink tub. Suddenly, the room was filled with bubbles.

I screamed for Bruce to no avail. I searched for anything—a door, anything. I stumbled onto the bed, then got back up. I waved my hands, trying to make a clear pathway to the outside door. Finding it, I started swooping up bubbles and taking them outside, throwing them out onto the black pavement.

It was dark now and the lighting was terrible. I continued to scream for Bruce. I heard the bathroom door open, and the fan stop.

"What happened, Sharon? Where are you?"

"I'll tell you later, just help me get this to stop and get this mess outside."

"Well, first of all, you have to turn the jets off."

"The jets?" I screamed. "Why didn't you tell me they were called jets?"

"Well, why would you buy bubble bath for a Jacuzzi?" he asked.

How did I know? "Just get this to stop!"

Suddenly, it became quiet.

The bubbles started to settle. We both looked at each other, neither knowing what to say.

Bruce spoke first. "Well, since you created this mess . . ."

"Yeah, I know. We need to clean up and we need towels to do it, and you probably want me to go get them."

He just looked at me, smile on his face and arms folded.

"OK, I will."

He came over and gave me a hug. "I should have told you about the buttons."

"It's OK," I said. "Let's get this mess cleaned up."

I headed to the office in search of towels, a little apprehensive to face the woman with the tuna fish sandwich. Instead, I was greeted by a long-legged, freckle-faced teen leaning on the counter, reading a *Superman* comic book. Clearly, he was offended by the disturbance. "If you are here about the fan, it's broke."

"Yeah, I know," I replied. "Hey, could I get some more towels?"

He looked back at his comic book. "I put towels in there this morning. I remember."

"Yeah, you did. Thank you, but I need more."

"Nobody else ever needs more." He looked at me accusingly.

"Well, we use a lot of towels."

"Why?"

"Look, how about a trade?"

"Are you going to steal 'em?"

"No, I won't steal them. I just want to make sure we leave everything super clean."

He nodded, as if that made sense. "What's your trade?" he asked. "I have to wash 'em."

"Well, I have some licorice sticks, a package of Oreos, and a *National Enquirer.*"

"Done!" he said, laying down his comics and going to the cupboard marked "Clean Towels." No dirty towels allowed in this closet.

After cleaning up the mess and wiping up the carpet, it seemed a few shades lighter than when I first saw it. We were both exhausted, and we'd had enough excitement for one night.

Leaving the money Bruce had saved for our Denny's breakfast, we headed home with a memory we would have least expected.

Petunia Soup

～

We lived in one of many cinder-block houses in a place called The Anchorage. The dwellings were built together in rows, with four apartments in each one. Next to each small entrance was a patch of dirt approximately three feet by three feet—this is where I played. With can and spoon in hand, I would spend many hours playing in the dirt.

A few doors down on the other side of the small area that separated the dwellings was an elderly man who had planted a beautiful and colorful petunia patch, which he had in his small area of dirt. My greatest joy as a five-year-old was to sit with him on his tiny step, eat a dish of ice cream, talk about his petunias, and many times go home with a small bouquet that my mother would put in a glass of water.

I began to go every day and loved sitting with Mr. Ed Evans, counting the number of petunias in each color. This became my happy space and something I looked forward to.

One day I went to the patch and Ed wasn't home. I sat on his step, thinking he would show up any minute, but he didn't. I looked at the beautiful patch and suddenly had an idea only a five-year-old would think of. I ran home, grabbed my soup can and my spoon from my patch of dirt. I then went in the house and poured the petunia water from the glass into my can and ran back to Ed's petunia patch.

I remember wondering if a petunia-patch soup would warm me up. I was always either hot or cold in our cinder-block dwelling. *I know*, I thought, *I will make petunia soup*. With that, I started pulling the petunia blossoms from their stems and filling my cup as the excess water sloshed over the edges. I packed them tightly, and by the time I was finished, I had left Ed's petunia patch starkly diminished of all the colors that made me happy. I looked in my can and then back at the patch. Something I hadn't felt before welled up inside of me. I was feeling a flush of guilt for the first time. I turned to run home, but when I looked up, Ed was standing in front of me with arms folded.

"Well, Sharon, you made short order of my petunias." He looked at my can and spoon as he said it. "Look in this can Sharon, what do you see?"

"Crushed up petunias." It was a messy conglomeration of distorted color.

"Just what is it you were trying to do?"

"I was gonna make petunia soup," I said, looking at the naked patch.

"Well, honey, this may be a good lesson for you. God blesses us in different ways with differ-ent things to make us happy." He motioned for me to sit down by him. "He gave us food, flowers, and sunshine, and he gave us ways to enjoy each one of the blessings that come our way. Food is meant to bring us comfort and make us strong. Sunshine makes us warm

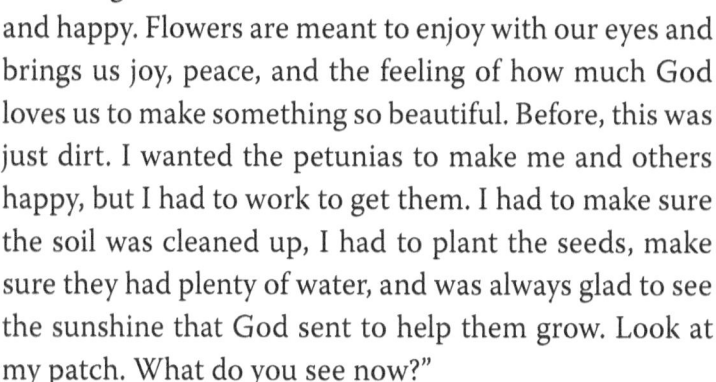

and happy. Flowers are meant to enjoy with our eyes and brings us joy, peace, and the feeling of how much God loves us to make something so beautiful. Before, this was just dirt. I wanted the petunias to make me and others happy, but I had to work to get them. I had to make sure the soil was cleaned up, I had to plant the seeds, make sure they had plenty of water, and was always glad to see the sunshine that God sent to help them grow. Look at my patch. What do you see now?"

"Nothing pretty," I replied.

"Those petunias in your can won't be good soup, honey. They are here to make us happy."

I looked at Ed and expected to see angry eyes, some-thing I was used to seeing at home. Instead, his eyes were soft with a look of concern that translated love to my five-year-old mind. I started to shiver. "Are you cold?"

Ed asked. I nodded. "How about I go in the house and bring us out some real soup." I nodded.

As we ate bowls of chicken noodle soup, I asked, "When will the petunias be back?"

"When we plant and love them," he said. "Eat your soup and run home before your mother calls."

I didn't understand all he was telling me, but I knew one thing for sure: I had learned many lessons, and one of them was forgiveness.

Mr. Oberndorfer

~

Good grades in junior high school were important to me. It was my way of being validated and recognized for a job well done. I wasn't the smartest kid, but I was ambitious and loved to learn.

The summer before my seventh-grade year started, I was seeing how far I could jump from our backyard swing, fell on my arm, and broke the bone at the shoulder. When my stepdad decided it was broken two days later, they took me to the doctor, who immediately sent me to surgery, where I had four long pins placed in the bone to have it heal back into the shoulder socket. I had a body cast that had two rods that kept my arm up and away from my body. Obviously, I couldn't start seventh grade on the first day. I was devastated.

Three months later, after having a homeschool teacher, the cast was removed, and I was sent to school. It was hard to adjust at first, but I finally found my way around and loved my teachers. The first class was Library. I found a book I remember to this day—*The Lion, the Witch and the Wardrobe,* by C. S. Lewis. This book mesmerized me, and I spent every free moment at home reading.

The only teacher who intimidated me was Mr. Oberndorfer, a very tall, slim middle-aged man who wore horn-rimmed glasses and maintained a very stoic persona. He taught geography, used a three-foot pointer at the blackboard, and seemed to have eyes in the back of his head. If someone wasn't paying attention or was talking, he would freeze in place at the blackboard, not moving a muscle. The sight was eerie and brought a sudden hush to the room. He would then proceed to teach us about the world around us, how natural resources are important, and other things that a seventh-grade student had no desire to learn about. I was one of those students. For some reason, I dismissed my homework in this class and let it slide, not thinking of the consequences.

I loved having school lunch. I don't know what happened financially for my parents, but they somehow had the money, and I no longer had to take my lunch to school.

The cooks would place huge bricks of real butter on each table. About twelve students could sit at a table and use as much butter as they wanted. I remember hot rolls straight from the oven being served every day. I would slather that fresh butter on my rolls and willingly took whatever the other students didn't want. I don't think the meals were very balanced, but I think the cooks did the best they could with what they knew. I remember having mashed potatoes and fish sticks with tartar sauce. The reason I remember this is because those two things were always my favorite. I was never a picky eater and always appreciated having my appetite satisfied.

When grades came out, we would take our report cards to the teacher when our names were called. Report-card day was usually special for me because getting good grades gave me validation and a certain degree of confidence that I otherwise didn't have.

When my grade was recorded, I would immediately look to see if the teacher had added any kind of note in the space provided. I often would see "Good job, Sharon," or Keep up the good work." This kind of validation sustained me for a long time and helped me want to work harder in the class.

However, Mr. Oberndorfer's geography class didn't get a lot of my attention. What's interesting about this is I never expected to get a bad grade.

Mr. Oberndorfer stood at the front of the class and seemed to stare a hole through all of us collectively. One would think the goal would be to do one's best in the class, but somehow as much as I was intimidated by him, I let my grade slide.

On report-card day, when my name was called, I took my card to the front and handed it to him. As he handed it back to me, I looked at my grade and immediately started crying. It wasn't just a cry, it was an outright sob. It was the biggest D grade imaginable. It dwarfed the As and Bs that were otherwise on my report card. I went to my desk, buried my head in my arms, and continued to sob, oblivious to the stares of my classmates.

I didn't look up until the first bell sounded for the next class and first lunch. I heard my name called.

I looked up. "Sharon," Mr. Oberndorfer said, "I need you to stay after for a few minutes." I immediately wiped my eyes and nose on the sleeve of my shirt.

I gathered my books and stood up. I was terrified. I stood there wishing I could fall through the floor. Better than that, I suddenly wished I could disappear into the magic land of Narnia with the Golden Lion, rescued from this horrible fate. If only I could have disappeared into that story right then.

I somehow made my way to the front of the class. I expected to see piercing eyes looking at me in disapproval. Mr. Oberndorfer took his glasses off and looked me straight in the eyes with the biggest strong yet gentle brown eyes. My rigid body softened immediately. He motioned for me to lay my books on the desk.

He folded his arms and slowly started to speak. His tone was totally different from the one he used while explaining continents, countries, and cultures. He talked slowly and with kindness. I found myself trusting him as I listened to his words.

"Sharon," he said, "I am not wanting to talk to you about your D grade. I do know you could have worked harder, however, and I am assured you know it too."

Now, having said that, he made sure I was listening to him. The outside hall noise was loud, and I felt myself leaning in. I had no idea what he was about to say, but I knew it was important. He had gotten past the part I was most worried about, and now I found myself curious about what was coming next.

"Sharon," he said, "first of all, I want you to know there is nothing wrong with showing your feelings."

I suddenly became aware of what a scene I must have made, breaking out in tears in front of all my classmates.

I gasped, and the embarrassment I felt was overwhelming. He obviously knew what I was feeling, and again he said, "There is nothing wrong with showing your feelings, Sharon. As I told you, I am not worried about your grade, but what does concern me is how some of your classmates are going to react to your tears."

I felt tears welling up in my eyes again . . . I knew what he was saying. There were certain classmates who I knew would be waiting to tease me and make fun of me.

It was as if he had read my mind. He went on to say, "When you leave this room, those students who mock you, point at you, and who are noticeably talking about you are not your friends. The last thing I want to happen is for them to make you cry again."

I wiped my eyes with the back of my hand, nodding in agreement.

"Do you know what you need to do when you leave this room and are faced with the backlash of your tears?"

I had to think about that word. I didn't know the definition, but my heart did.

"Be strong," I said. I didn't say it as a question, but as a statement.

He looked at me and smiled, nodding his head. "That's right. Throughout your life, you will be faced with many decisions regarding how you interact with those around you. You will also learn about how you treat other people and how they will respond to you. The most important message I want you to learn from this is to be strong and to be kind. He then handed me my books. "You need to go now. I think they are serving fish sticks and tartar sauce today."

He raised his eyebrows when he said that.

Wow! I thought. *I know something about Mr. Oberndorfer that no one else does. He loves fish sticks and tartar sauce.*

I left that room with my head held high.

It's What's Inside That Counts

~

As a sophomore in high school, I had absolutely no social skills. My stepfather was unemployed much of the time, and our family suffered because of it. When I turned sixteen, I immediately looked for a job and found one working at a nursing home for elderly people struggling with memory loss.

Many of my friends were candy stripers, the name for young girls who volunteered at hospitals, nursing homes, and other facilities. Much to my delight, the owner of this nursing home never even asked me about it. After working there for only a few days, I could see why. The owner was a hard-headed woman who went around with a cigarette hanging from her mouth, unkept bright red hair and a deep, booming voice she would use occasionally with some of the unruly patients. She walked around in a men's muscle shirt, with a live monkey on her shoulder that screeched incessantly—you can't make this up. She lived in a one-room apartment adjacent to the nursing home. She scared me to death.

Because there were no modern conveniences back then, I spent a lot of my time in the laundry room, washing and folding adult diapers. I worked after school and on weekends. The money I earned went to help contribute whatever I could for my four younger brothers. Sometimes it was something like a coat for one of them, and maybe a loaf of bread.

My stepfather refused to ask for help from anyone. Because money was scarce, for lunch I would go to the canteen on the lower level of the high school and buy me a candy bar every day.

I loved the classes I took and found validation in doing well at school. The social part of school was intimidating. I would walk against the outside wall of the halls, head down and always determined not to look any of my classmates in the eyes, ever.

My favorite class was history. I would go in as soon as the bell would ring. My class before history was just next door, so I was always in my seat a few minutes before the second bell rang. The most popular boy in the entire sophomore class would come in and always draw the attention of all the other students in the class. He appeared confident, authoritative, and self-absorbed, demanding attention, which he always received from the other students. He sat directly in front of me, and I was happy to just be ignored completely by him.

That is, until one day . . . Without any warning whatsoever, he took his seat, turned around, and scanned my face. "Well," he said, "you'd be pretty cute if you weren't so fat."

I felt my breath catch in my throat, and my first thought went to the candy bar I had for lunch every day. I wished I hadn't. He turned back around, and class started.

For days, I could think of nothing else but the scathing comment from the most popular boy in the sophomore class. For days, maybe weeks—I can't remember—I could barely look myself in the mirror.

I don't know if I talked to anyone about it—I doubt it—but there was a turning point, and it was the beginning of how I viewed myself from then on.

One morning, I looked in the mirror and I didn't see fat, I didn't see insecure, I didn't see lack of self-confidence. Instead, I saw determination! Sheer determination. I don't know where it came from, but that day was the beginning of the rest of my life. I can't say everything changed at once. It didn't. It was like baby steps.

I went to school and started walking closer to the middle of the hallway. Still raising my head only to see where I was going, I mostly kept my eyes on my feet.

This went on for a while, and then something happened I never expected—I heard my name being said by a few of the students as we made our way to each of our classes. "Hey, Sharon," "Hi, Sharon," "Nice hair, Sharon." My hair was very long, and I never thought of it as nice, but someone thought it was.

Eventually, I looked up as someone said my name and I would raise my hand to say hi, and with time, I was able to smile and return the greeting.

I remember how good I started to feel and actually looked forward to school. Nothing changed at home, but the acceptance I was receiving was changing my life. What I didn't realize was that acceptance was always there. I just needed to recognize it.

So often we become so self-absorbed that we don't realize others are there ready to accept and love us for who we are.

I loved the new me. The confident sixteen-year-old who actually felt liked and accepted by my peers.

The following year at school, my junior year, I was voted in as a member of the student council, I was part of the drama club, and had a lead part in the school play. My senior year, I made it to the marching team, where only fifty girls were chosen out of several hundred. I had my good days and my bad days. However, I learned that what I put into the lives of others very often would come back into my own.

With that confidence, I decided to ask for a raise from my scary employer. I found out I was being paid much less than what I felt I was worth. She refused, so I quit and actually found a better job car hopping, where smiling brought me big tips.

I still don't like monkeys, though.

Elephant Camp

~

When I started telling this story to my TikTok "grand-children," I wasn't sure where it came from. Either I was told it as a child, or maybe a schoolteacher had been the source. Wherever it came from, I feel it is full of important messages. It is a great metaphor that represents the burdens we may carry from not thinking we are enough. It represents the "ropes" that can easily be broken if we will just have the faith to move forward and believe in ourselves.

There was a man who loved elephants. He loved them so much, he decided he wanted to visit an elephant camp where they were being trained for the circus.

As he began to walk through the camp, he saw all ages, sizes, and shapes. The elephants all seemed to be taken care of properly, with enough water to drink, food to eat, and cleanliness in each of their areas. However, as he looked closer, he noticed something very peculiar. No matter the size of the beast, there was a small rope tied to the ankle just above the foot. The rope extended a short distance and attached to a stake that had been hammered in the ground to hold the rope.

Something else he noticed that he found peculiar: The smaller elephants were repeatedly backing up in an attempt to free themselves from the rope attached to the stake in the ground.

Being small, no matter how each one tried, they could not free themselves.

The older elephants had the same-size rope attached to the same-size stake. The rope and stake could have been easily pulled from the ground if they had just moved back. Instead, they stayed, fixating their gazes to the ground. The man couldn't help but think the huge elephants appeared to look defeated and disheartened.

Watching for a while, he couldn't understand for the life of him why the huge elephants didn't just back up. That would free them immediately from the rope and the bond that was holding them back. Finally, unable to understand the reasoning, he went to the trainer, who was reloading the water buckets and feed bins.

"I have a question for you," he said.

The trainer looked up while staying with his task.

"Why is it," the man said, "the bigger elephants are letting those small ropes hold them? I can see why the smaller elephants are not able to move away even with their best efforts. Clearly the ropes are strong enough to hold them. But the big elephants? They could snap those ropes by simply stepping back."

The trainer set his water hose down and turned it off, making sure he had not missed any of the elephant stalls.

"Well," he said, "you see, we are training the elephants to stay in place when we need them to do so. When they come to us, we put a rope around their leg strong enough to hold them. Although they try and try to break those ropes, they are unsuccessful. When they reach maturity, it is then they are strong enough. By that time, they have lost their will to try."

Many of these ropes are the result of past hurts. Perhaps we've been told we aren't pretty enough, or we're not smart enough, and as a result, we lack confidence and self-worth. We can't imagine moving on because someone has told us we would never be able to progress from our current status in life. Perhaps we have told ourselves we don't have the ability to move on, to progress, to reach our full potential.

Break those ropes! Believe in yourself! You are a divinely made, incredible human being with potential just waiting to be discovered.

Break those ropes! Move ahead and become the person God has intended for you to be.

Why? Because you *can* . . . that's why!

Farmer Dan

~

I taught in the school district on and off for about twenty years as a substitute teacher. Every class I ever taught heard this story. I'm not even sure where it came from, but I continued to carry it on with my TikTok "grandchildren." It is one of my most favorite metaphoric stories I have ever heard.

Farmer Dan lived in a little farming community. The land he farmed was on the outskirts. He loved to plant, weed, and harvest on this little acreage and was always seen on his tractor working. Whatever the season, he was out there on that rich soil, doing whatever needed to be done for that time of year. He was easy to spot, as his acreage ran adjacent to the only road that came in and out of that little town. When he was facing the road, he could see everyone coming and going. He knew everyone's name and also what kind of vehicle they drove. He always waved to the passersby.

Farmer Dan was a strange one. If you liked a guy who didn't beat around the bush, he was the guy for you. Straightforward and honest.

One spring morning as he was planting tomatoes, he was looking back, making sure his rows were straight, and heard a car driving in the direction of town. He could tell without even looking up from which the direction the cars were coming. If he couldn't look toward the road, he still managed to be able to raise his arm and wave. This time, looking back at his tomato rows, he had one hand on the steering wheel of his big red tractor and raised his other arm, his hand waving vigorously. Yes indeed, Farmer Dan was quite a guy.

He heard the vehicle pull over to the side of the road. *This must be important,* he thought.

Being farther out in the field, he had to squint his eyes to see. *That's strange,* he thought, as he saw someone getting out of the car.

"That's really strange," he said out loud, as it was a car he didn't recognize.

"Well, I'll be darned," he said, out loud. "This must be purty important."

Farmer Dan never turned his tractor off in the middle of planting, but off it went. He got off and started walking toward the stranger.

"Howdy," he said, tipping his well-weathered straw hat. Squinting his eyes and still not recognizing the person, he moved forward.

"What can I do fer ya?" he asked.

"Well," the person replied, "I'm thinking about moving into your community."

Farmer Dan was known not to reply until he heard all the details. He folded his arms, grabbed a shoot of straw, put it in his mouth, squinted his eyes, and waited to hear more.

The visitor continued, "Before I make the move, I have a question."

Farmer Dan nodded, prompting the person to continue.

"I'd like to know what kind of people live here. Are they courteous, helpful, friendly, kind? Are they compassionate, understanding?"

Farmer Dan continued to listen without saying a word.

The person went on. "Do they make good friends? Are they loyal?"

When Farmer Dan could see the person was finished, he looked this stranger straight in the eye and replied, "That's a mighty long list."

The person nodded, apparently quite proud of the accomplishment.

"Well, my friend," Farmer Dan said, "before I answer ya, let me ask you a question."

The person nodded in agreement.

"Tell me about the community y'all are comin' from . . . Are the people there courteous, helpful, friendly, kind, and all them other things y'all are looking for?"

The person didn't even hesitate. "Absolutely not," was the answer. "They aren't friendly at all. I wouldn't trust any of them as far as I could throw them, and as far as being dependable?" The person let out a loud "Ha!," followed by an "Absolutely not!"

"Well, my friend . . ." Farmer Dan stopped, took the straw out of his mouth, and looked the person straight in the eye.

"Well, my friend," he said again, "those are the same kind of people you will find in this community."

With that, the person turned sharply and headed towards the car, jumped in, spun that car around, and took off in the other direction.

Farmer Dan wiped his forehead with his kerchief and said out loud, "Pretty warm out here for a day in May." Got back on his tractor and began planting those big, beautiful Early Girl tomato plants, all the time thinking of those delicious tomato sandwiches he'd be enjoying come harvest time.

A few weeks later, Farmer Dan would be seen on his tractor planting the rest of his crops. Planting seeds for a hearty crop of beets, one of his favorites, he was thinking of those delicious pickled beets he'd be enjoying at harvest time when he noticed something very peculiar.

A car had pulled over to the side of his property and a person was getting out. He squinted his eyes to take a better look. *Well, that's strange,* he thought.

Being farther out in the field, he had to take a second look. "That's really strange," he said out loud, as he saw someone getting out of a car he didn't recognize.

This must be purty important, he thought. He watched as the person started toward him, walking on his freshly planted rows. He jumped from his tractor. "Hey, you can't walk on my plants," he yelled.

The person stopped abruptly.

Farmer Dan continued toward the stranger. Tipping his hat, he said, "Fresh planted . . . What can I do fer y'all?"

"Well," the person said, "I'm thinking about moving

into your community."

Farmer Dan pulled a pickin' of straw from the beautiful rich soil, put it in his mouth, and didn't say a thing, but kept looking that stranger straight in the eyes.

Farmer Dan was known for his undivided attention, which some people found to be a little intimidating.

The person went on. "Before I make a decision, I have a question for ya, since you're the only one I've seen so far from this town. You are from this town, right?"

"Sure am," Farmer Dan replied, never taking his eyes off the person.

"Well, I have a question."

Farmer Dan nodded.

"Before I move into this town, I would like to know what the people are like . . ."

He continued, realizing Farmer Dan was waiting for more. Farmer Dan never made a quick reply and always gave people the chance to finish all they had to say. "Well, the visitor went on. "I don't want to move here until I find out what the people are like. Are they friendly, helpful, courteous, kind? Are they compassionate, understanding?"

Farmer Dan continued to listen without saying a word.

The person went on. "Do they make good friends? Are they loyal?"

When Farmer Dan could see the person was finished, he looked this stranger straight in the eye and replied, "That's a mighty long list."

The person nodded.

"Well, my friend," Farmer Dan said, "before I answer ya, let me ask you a question."

The person nodded in agreement.

"What are the people like in the community you are coming from? Are they friendly, helpful, courteous, kind?"

The person didn't hesitate. "Oh yes! They are all of those things. It's a great community, and I love the people."

"Well, my friend," Farmer Dan went on, "those are the exact kind of people you will find in this community."

Both smiled. Farmer Dan went back to his tractor, admiring the planted rows and thinking how good those pickled beets would taste!

The Weatherworn Bouquet

*B*eing a young mother in the '60s was challenging, especially with three little ones under foot. Money was scarce since we had just purchased a home, and entertainment was mostly experienced in church activities, getting together with neighbors for potlucks, working in our garden, and shopping at the nearby market.

My husband worked long hours and usually got home after the children were in bed.

One Saturday afternoon, we dropped the kids off to Grandma's house and went for a ride in our yellow Volkswagen Bug. This car was transportation for all five of us. The kids would pile into the back seat, telling us to please drive over the railroad tracks, which would toss them up, their heads hitting the ceiling of the car slightly. Because there were no seat belts, precautions were taken by loading the kids in the car and telling them to sit down and be quiet. Naturally, this never worked. So being able to take a drive without the kids was always a treat.

This day, after we dropped the kids off, we headed up the road, our destination being the Arctic Circle for ice cream—vanilla or chocolate, or even my favorite twist cone. We traveled on the one road leading in and out of our small town. On either side were open fields of alfalfa, hay, sugar beets, and tomatoes. Being springtime, the fields spread out in wild grass and flowers. It was a sight to behold, and one I took for granted.

As we headed east, Bruce suddenly jerked the car over to the right side of the two-lane highway and stopped short with a jerk. Completely taken by surprise, I held on for dear life. When I was finally able to get my wits about me and was composed enough to talk, I screamed, "What's wrong?" I looked over and saw the brightest, most mischievous smile on Bruce's face. I just looked at him with my mouth wide open. We were going at least thirty miles per hour and I had no clue as to why the sudden, jerky stop along the side of the road.

As I was still contemplating what the smile was all about when we could have easily died, he jumped from the car and ran around the other side toward the field, where the barbed wire had broken down, providing an opening between the posts. He literally propelled himself across that broken barbed wire and, strangely, looked back at me with a quick smile as he continued to run crazily into the open field. He always was saying how the kids were driving him bonkers, and it had finally happened. I was sure he had lost his mind.

He came to a sudden stop in front of a wild yellow rosebush. He carefully picked off several of the prickly stemmed blossoms and made his way back to the car. Before entering, he took out his pocketknife and removed the prickles. Opening the door, he settled in his seat and handed me the bouquet of slightly weather-worn wild yellow roses that to this day remain the most beautiful bouquet I have ever received. Being a man of little words, the smile on his face clearly delivered the message to my heart.

The Magic of a Smile
~

uses in Salt Lake City in the '60s were either early, late, or didn't come at all. Many people took the bus because of the convenience and low fare, in spite of sometimes arriving late or too early to their destinations. I usually took two buses and had to wait or miss both.

I decided finally to arrive at my bus stops early and just take the chance of having to wait for my classes to start. I was attending a business college in Salt Lake City, and would take my first bus from home and then spend time waiting for my second bus to arrive to deliver me to my school.

I decided since I had to wait, I would observe the other people waiting as well, and soon found it to be an interesting pastime.

People at my bus stop came from all walks of life. All very bland in their expressions. No one was going to appear excited having to wait at a bus stop. However, I found myself watching their expressions and found some to seem tired, others irritated, some neutral, and I even observed some happy expressions.

One day, a new person arrived at the bus stop who clearly had a sad expression on his face. An older man of medium height and slight build, wearing a blue ball cap pulled over his eyes, approached my bus stop. It wasn't the expression on his face that struck me as being sad as much as it was the way he carried himself.

Sadness can be felt. It's an energy that most all of us can pick up on. I felt it. I couldn't see his whole face because he had his head lowered and the ball cap covered his eyes. But the sense of sadness I felt from him seemed natural. I began watching him for a few days and forgot about all the others with their varied expressions.

I finally felt this man needed a friend. I couldn't be a real friend, but maybe I could be someone who would make his day just a little bit better.

After this decision, I started saying good morning to him as brightly and kindly as I could. No response. I thought at first he might be deaf, but then realized he could hear me. I saw him look at me through the corners of his eyes.

I persisted. After a week or so, I moved a little closer and gave him the brightest smile I could with a heartfelt good morning.

Some days, I didn't feel it was a good morning and I didn't feel like smiling, but I continued each morning at that bus stop with the same plan of action. Interestingly, I had no expectations other than to make sure this man knew someone cared.

I almost decided to give up, when one morning I thought I saw him tip his hat at me. *Progress*, I thought. *This is progress.*

I have found throughout my life that one of my innate characteristics is persistence. I have found my persistence to be good and bad. In a positive light, it has helped me achieve my goals and overcome obstacles, and lots of times it has helped in my personal life. However, my persistence has had many faces. One of them I have tried hard to overcome is stubbornness. But I don't think stubbornness was a part of what I wanted to achieve in my goal to help this sad man to feel better at least for a few minutes. I think if I had seen any kind of irritation coming from him, I would have stopped trying.

He showed up every morning, wearing a slightly worn lightweight jacket that seemed too thin for the cool weather on a chilly February morning in Salt Lake City. He always carried a folded-up brown paper sack, which I decided must be his lunch.

I persisted.

Then one morning, something happened I never would have expected. I had approached him a little closer, always certain not to invade his personal space but still make sure he heard my greeting and saw my smile even if it was from the corner of his eye. That morning, he looked up at me and I saw a faint smile in return. I was ecstatic. My persistence had paid off.

I didn't see a reaction for a while after that. Then one day when I had had a very difficult morning, I almost decided I really, really didn't feel like smiling. My day had started off horribly. It was a Monday, and the Saturday before I had been stood up for a date. I was so humiliated, and it was still lingering on as my potential bus stop friend approached. I was still contemplating my bad mood and wondered if I could even make a sincere attempt at a smile and a good-morning greeting.

As I stood there still wondering if I wanted to change my attitude and continue my goal, he approached me. He raised his blue ball cap upward, and I saw tired older eyes that clearly looked sad to me. I saw a smile across his face, and his tired eyes looked at me with kindness that I can still feel to this day when I think about it.

He then spoke words that have stayed with me for decades. "I just want to thank you for your good-morning greeting." He went on. "And I especially want to thank you for your smile. It's the only one I get all day."

"Thank you," I said. "I hope it makes your day better."

"It makes my day," he said.

The bus arrived and we both boarded on our way to our destinations. I smiled all day. Somehow, the disappointment of my date who stood me up didn't seem to matter anymore.

The Butterfly Story

~

This is one of my favorite stories. Its depth and meaning spans generations and is relatable to all ages. I've tried to remember where I first heard it, but it's one of those stories that could have come from any one of a myriad of people over my lifetime. Its message is one of love but profoundly offers a word of caution, as well. Care . . . but don't carry.

A grandfather was taking his grandson to see a flower garden as he had become old enough to appreciate its beauty. He pointed out the variety of colors and the sweet fragrances that permeated the fresh summer air. He pointed out the different shapes and contours of each unique blossom. He turned around to see where the boy's interest was directed and found him kneeling down on the stone walkway looking at something very intently.

"Look, Grandfather," he said.

The grandfather looked down to find the boy's attention was on a butterfly chrysalis that had fallen to the ground. The grandfather saw a wonderful opportunity to explain how it would soon be a beautiful butterfly as the boy cried out, "Grandpa, its struggling! We need to help it!"

With that, the boy reached down with a tiny twig to open the chrysalis.

"No," the grandfather said quietly. "The butterfly's struggles will make it stronger. It will be fine and will turn into a colorful butterfly with strong wings." Seeing that his words had no effect on the boy's actions, he watched as the butterfly came out with limp, withered wings hanging at its side. The boy looked up in surprise and dismay.

The grandfather looked back knowing in his heart that his grandson would learn a hard but helpful lesson from this very sad experience. He called him by name and said, "You have learned a difficult lesson from this. Because you did not let it struggle in doing something it should do by itself—something that would make its wings strong and healthy—the butterfly may never fly. I understand how difficult it was to watch, but it was what needed to happen. You need to know now that it's the struggles that make "us" stronger.

This story is one that resonates with us in a way that is both helpful and hard. We want to help those we love in any way we can. However, many of us tend to consume all the responsibilities of those we love who can make it on their own. We need to remember that struggling makes us stronger; better equipped to meet the challenges that will continue to be a part of our lives.

Care . . . but don't carry.

Change Is Hard

~

My husband once made me feel so safe, like everything was somehow always going to be okay. He was my solid ground, my refuge, a dependable constant throughout any uncertainty.

Since he has been sick these last seventeen months, my life has taken a turn. Having the privilege of being his caregiver is something I wouldn't change. That is the way I prefer it. The biggest eye opener is that I never realized he did so much. I kind of took it for granted.

The reason I tell you this is because I want to stress the importance of gratitude, the importance of making sure we express our gratitude to those who do even the smallest things for us. Also, I want to express the need to never take anything for granted, to know change is inevitable, and to know that through it all, everything is going to be OK. No, you are never alone. God is in the heavens. There is always someone to help, even if you don't think so. God will put them in your path. Move forward, be productive, be happy, and adjust to your circumstances. You can because . . .

"YOU CAN DO HARD THINGS"

Poetry

Friends

~

Special people
Who seldom know
By their loving examples
They are helping and encouraging
Others to grow
They stand out
And gently show the way
By the things they do
And the words they say

God Never Left Us

~

In my earlier years, I worked in a very stressful environment and often found myself driving home agitated, anxious and out of sorts. One evening after I had to work a couple of hours overtime, I was on my way home and saw something I hadn't noticed before. A beautiful sunset filled with gold, blue, and especially pink hues of beautiful color stretching like lightning bolts in all directions. I was taken aback, so I pulled the car over to the side of the road, got out, leaned on the hood, and truly practiced a form of mindfulness I hadn't remembered experiencing before. This poem was written not long after.

A beautiful sunset . . .
A beautiful sight . . .
Reminding us of God's
Wondrous light.
The day soon to be over
With a new day to begin.
As the soft light of daybreak
Reminds us again.
God never left us . . .
He watches with care . . .
And as the new day begins
He will always be there.

Mother's Garden

~

If I planted a garden and added a flower
For each time you've been there
For me . . . for every hour . . .
The world would be paved with
Flowers, galore.
There wouldn't be room to
Plant any more.

Spirit to Spirit

Spirit to Spirit has been shared more times than I can count. Looking back, I wish I had kept a record of all the spiritual experiences I have had in sharing this. Whenever I saw a young mother with a baby in her arms, I would be moved to ask if I could read my poem to her.

One Christmas Eve, in 1998, I felt a need to go to the mall—maybe for a card I had forgotten—I didn't know whose it was, but I still felt moved to go. As I entered the Hallmark store, I saw a clerk at the counter, and a young woman in one of the aisles. Immediately, I felt her sadness and was prompted to approach her. I hesitated, but again was prompted to reach out.

I walked up to her and asked her if she would mind if I recited a poem I had written. Her pain was palpable, and I knew I was doing the right thing. Upon finishing *Spirit to Spirit*, she told me the story of how her three-year-old little girl who could not speak or hear had just passed away. She thanked me with a hug and asked if she could send me a Christmas card.

A few days later, I received the following card in the mail:

Dear Sharon,

Words can not describe the feelings I had as you recited "Spirit to Spirit" last Friday night, a night that I will never forget. You allowed my Kelsey to show her love and express herself to me in a way that was never possible for her when she was here with us.

Thank you for being our angel and making this a special Christmas!

This has been a precious memory and shows how God blesses us in mysterious and unexpected ways.

Dear little child, what words will I know . . .
To teach you, reach you,
Help you to grow?
How will I teach you by words, alone,
As the language of angels is all you have known?
I will look in your eyes with concern and love,
While asking for wisdom from our Father, above.
Our spirits will speak . . . though no words will be said.
And by the
"Power of love"
You will gently be led.

The Sunflower

~

Living in what was once a rural community, we had plenty of open fields, wildflowers, and dirt paths to enjoy. For about ten years, I owned a small publishing company and had the opportunity to sell my poetry and photography in picture frames I had designed to a well-known Utah publisher. One early morning while walking down a dirt path, camera in hand, I came across this sunflower that had somehow risen from the center of a densely grown sweet-pea bush. I stopped in my tracks, knowing I was seeing somewhat of an anomaly. How, I wondered, did that single magnificent sunflower find its way there? I took a picture and wrote this poem.

The Sunflower

As I took my walk that morning,
the white, puffy clouds hung lazily in the azure sky.
Among the summer splendor, something caught my eye.
A sunflower tall, majestic, full of life, had grown up
within the middle of the wild sweet peas,
a journey filled with challenges and strife.
Dark and cold with obstacles galore,
the sunflower rose by inches above that dark, damp dirt floor.
Determined there was hope, the sunflower grew on
Inching its way above the earth
faithfully hoping to find the warm and glowing sun.
It made its way!
You will, too!
Don't let challenges discourage you!
Find your way! I know you can! Have faith! Stay strong!
And you, too, will find that warm and glowing sun!

You Can Weather the Storms of Life

~

When the storms of life get you down . . .
remember . . . after each one
a rainbow is found. So, weather the storms!
Don't let hopelessness win.
A rainbow is coming with a new day to begin.

EVERY DAY REMIND YOURSELF

"YOU CAN DO HARD THINGS"

Angels

~

I wrote the *Angels* poem over thirty years ago. It is the poem most of my TikTok Grandchildren will remember the most. Many of them have loved ones they have lost and have come to my TikTok livestream for comfort.

I, as well, have loved ones who have passed, and at times have felt their presence.

I believe we communicate with our "angels" through our spirits and our hearts. This poem is particularly special to me for that reason.

If you believe in angels
If you believe they are real
It won't be what you see or hear—instead it's what you'll feel.
On days that are most difficult with no one else around
You will feel angels helping you
Although you will not see them
Nor will you hear a sound!

"Simply Delicious" Recipes

Apple and Pineapple Crisp

~

Ingredients

4 cups peeled, sliced apples (any kind)
1 (8-ounce) can crushed pineapple
1 tablespoon lemon juice
¾ cup packed brown sugar
¾ cup oats
1 teaspoon ground cinnamon
1 teaspoon ground nutmeg
½ cup chopped pecans
⅓ cup melted butter

Instructions

Preheat oven to 350°F. Arrange apples in a 9×9-inch baking dish sprayed with nonstick coating. Mix undrained pineapple and lemon juice. Spread over apples. Combine brown sugar, spices, oats, and pecans in a bowl and mix well. Stir in melted butter. Sprinkle over prepared layers. Bake covered with foil for 30 minutes. Remove foil. Bake 10 to 12 minutes more or until crisp. Serve alone or with whipped cream or ice cream.

Ann Ford's Crunch Cookies

~

Ann is one of the loveliest friends I have met on TikTok. Faced with a myriad of health problems, she still finds the time to share her positivity. When I first "met" her indirectly, I loved her immediately—and I really love her crunch cookie recipe, which, incidentally, came from her mother. Ann is in her seventies, so this could definitely be called a multigenerational recipe!

Ingredients

1 cup white sugar

1 cup brown sugar

1 cup butter

1 cup corn oil

1 egg

1 teaspoon salt

1 teaspoon vanilla

1 teaspoon baking soda

1 teaspoon cream of tartar

3½ cups all-purpose flour

1 cup Rice Krispies

1 cup shredded coconut

1 cup oatmeal

1 cup nuts

Instructions

Preheat oven to 350°F. Cream together first 7 ingredients. Add soda, cream of tartar, and flour; mix well. Add Rice Krispies, coconut, oatmeal, and nuts. Roll mixture into balls. Place on ungreased cookie sheet. Bake for about 10 minutes. I made this recipe not realizing it would make a ton of cookies—11 dozen. I gave them out for two days.

Cheesecake Bars

When I ran across this recipe in an old recipe book I found in a thrift store, I wondered if it would be good . . . it was! Years ago, the food resources were just not available to make "fancy" food!

Ingredients

⅓ cup butter or margarine
½ cup brown sugar
1 cup flour

½ cup walnuts or pecans, chopped
¼ cup sugar

1 egg
2 tablespoons milk
1 tablespoons lemon juice
½ teaspoon vanilla or almond extract
8-ounce cream cheese

Instructions

Preheat oven to 350°F. Cream together butter, brown sugar, flour, and nuts. Reserve 1 cup for topping. Press into an 8-inch square pan. Bake for 12 to 15 minutes. Blend sugar, cream cheese, egg, milk, lemon juice, and vanilla. Beat well and spread over baked crust. Sprinkle with reserved crumbs. Bake for an additional 25 minutes. Refrigerate for at least 2 hours and up to 12 hours.

Chicken Stuffed Crescent Rolls

Ingredients

1 (10.5-ounce) can cream of chicken soup
¼ cup milk
1 tablespoon sour cream
½ cup grated cheese
2 cups cooked, seasoned, cubed chicken
1 can crescent rolls (8 count)

Instructions

Preheat oven to 350°F. Mix first three ingredients together. Spread half of soup mixture on bottom of baking dish. Open rolls. Put 1 tablespoon of chicken, dollop of soup mixture, and cheese on the large part of the triangle and roll up. Place in baking dish. Pour remaining soup mixture evenly on top. Bake for 30–35 minutes, until golden brown.

Christmas Pudding

~

This is a Christmas pudding recipe that was introduced to me by my mother-in-law fifty-eight years ago. When I watched her make it, I was wondering how on earth a pudding could taste good with potatoes and carrots. It has been a favorite of my family for decades.

Ingredients

1 cup grated carrots	½ cup raisins
1 teaspoon baking soda	½ cup butter, melted
1 cup grated potatoes	¼ teaspoon ground cloves
1 cup sugar	¼ teaspoon cinnamon
1 cup flour	¼ teaspoon nutmeg

Instructions

Stir baking soda into grated carrots and potatoes. Mix all ingredients together. Fill two #2 size cans ½ full. Cover tightly with aluminum foil and tie with a string to secure it from leaking. Steam 3 hours.

Sauce Ingredients

2 tablespoons cornstarch
¼ cup water
1 pint water
½ cup sugar
3 tablespoons butter
Dash of nutmeg
Pinch of salt
Zest and juice of one lemon

Sauce Instructions

Start with 2 tablespoons corn starch and ¼ cup water and mix until dissolved. Set aside. In a medium pot, add 1 pint water, sugar, and butter and bring to a boil. Slowly drizzle in the cornstarch and water mixture, stirring constantly until desired thickness. Add a dash of nutmeg and a pinch of salt. Add lemon zest and juice. Pour over pudding.

Crispy Garlic Chicken

~

Because I looked for recipes that are "simply delicious," this especially stood out as one that would be just that—simple and delicious.

Ingredients

¼ cup parmesan cheese
1 envelope onion soup mix
8 uncooked chicken tenders
3 tablespoons plain breadcrumbs

Instructions

Preheat oven to 400°F. In medium bowl, combine soup mix, mayonnaise, and cheese. On baking sheet, arrange chicken and top with mixture. Sprinkle all over with breadcrumbs. Bake 20 minutes. Eat and enjoy!

Dinner in a Hurry

This recipe is one I have made when I am in a hurry. It's fast, easy, and "simply delicious."

Ingredients

1 pound ground beef
1 (10.5-ounce) can of cream of mushroom soup
1 (14.5-ounce) can of tomatoes with juice
½ cup long-grain white rice
¾ cup shredded mozzarella cheese
Salt and pepper to taste

Instructions

Crumble the ground beef in a skillet over medium-high heat. Salt and pepper to taste. Cook and stir until evenly browned. Drain off grease, if necessary. Stir in cream of mushroom soup, tomatoes, and uncooked rice. Cover and simmer over low heat, stirring occasionally until rice is cooked—about 15 minutes. Preheat broiler. When the rice is done, transfer the contents into a casserole dish. Cover with a layer of cheese. Broil until cheese is melted. Enjoy!

Double Delicious Cookies

This is my favorite holiday cookie. The recipe came from a community cookbook that was a compilation of favorite recipes from different women in our neighborhood about fifty years ago. Be careful . . . these cookies will go fast. Make sure you get one before they are all gone.

Ingredients

1 stick (½ cup) butter
½ cup graham cracker crumbs
1 (14-ounce) can sweetened condensed milk
1 (12-ounce) package semisweet chocolate chips
1 cup Reese's Peanut Butter Chips

Instructions

Preheat oven to 325°F. Melt butter in oven in a 9×13-inch baking dish. Sprinkle crumbs evenly over melted butter. Pour condensed milk evenly over crumbs. Top with chips and press firmly. Bake 25 minutes or until lightly browned. Cool in refrigerator for a couple of hours before cutting into bars. Store loosely covered at room temperature. Yummm!

Taco Salad

Bruce and I spent fifteen months living in Quincy, Illinois. We were treated to this delicious and easy taco salad, which has become a favorite of ours for over seventeen years.

Ingredients

1 head of lettuce
1 cup of seasoned ground beef
1 small bottle of Catalina salad dressing
Plain nacho corn chips
1–2 Fresh tomatoes

Instructions

Cook and season ground beef. Let cool to room temperature. Separate and break lettuce in bite-size pieces. Cut tomatoes in bite-size pieces. Toss in a large bowl. Add dressing. Gently crush corn chips. Mix in with salad. Serve.

Easy Apple Pie

~

Ingredients

1 can biscuits (8 count)
4 apples peeled, cored, and diced
¾ cup sugar
2 teaspoons lemon juice
1 teaspoon cinnamon
3 tablespoons cornstarch
½ cup water
½ cup melted butter

Cinnamon-Sugar Mixture

½ cup brown sugar
2 teaspoons cinnamon
¼ teaspoon nutmeg

Icing

1 cup powdered sugar
2 tablespoons milk
½ teaspoons vanilla

Instructions

Preheat oven to 350°F. Combine the lemon juice, 1 teaspoon of cinnamon, white sugar, cornstarch, and apples in a saucepan. Cook over medium heat and stir occasionally. When the apple mixture starts to thicken up, add a half cup of water. Stir and continue cooking for ten minutes. Set aside. In small bowl, mix brown sugar, cinnamon, and nutmeg. Dip the biscuits in the brown sugar mixture on both sides. Place in skillet and pour on the rest of the butter. Sprinkle on the rest of the cinnamon mixture. Spoon apple mixture on top. Bake for 45 minutes.

Funeral Potatoes

These potatoes are served usually at funeral lunches, especially in the culture of the Church of Jesus Christ. The Church believes that when people pass on they are stepping through a "door" into a continued and happy life where they serve as angels to help those they love who remain on Earth.

Ingredients

30 ounces diced or shredded hash browns, thawed
2 cups sour cream
1 (10.5-ounce) can cream of chicken soup
10 tablespoons butter, divided and melted
1 teaspoon salt
¼ teaspoon freshly ground black pepper
1 teaspoon dried minced onion
2 cups shredded cheddar cheese
2 cups cornflakes cereal

Instructions

(Allow potatoes to thaw in your fridge overnight, or spread them on a baking sheet and warm them in the oven at 200°F for about 20 minutes, until thawed). Preheat oven to 350°F. Combine sour cream, cream of chicken soup, 6 tablespoons of melted butter, salt, pepper, and dried onion in a bowl. Mix well. Add potatoes and shredded cheese and stir to combine. Spoon mixture into a single layer in a 9×13-inch pan. Add cornflakes to a large Ziploc bag and crush gently with your hands or a rolling pin. Add remaining 4 tablespoons of melted butter to the crushed cornflakes and combine well. Sprinkle mixture over potatoes. Bake uncovered for 40–50 minutes.

Let's Make a Fruit Salad

~

This recipe was found in an old recipe book. I made a TikTok while making it and had 3,434 likes. I hope everyone who made it enjoyed it as much as we did.

This is probably one of the easiest fruit salads you will ever make, and it is "simply delicious."

Ingredients

1 (6-ounce) can of pineapple chunks
1 (11-ounce) can of mandarin oranges
10 ounces of fresh blueberries
2 cups of red grapes
1 pound of coarsely chopped fresh strawberries
1 small packet (3-ounce) of plain vanilla instant pudding
1½ teaspoons vanilla

Instructions

Combine all the fruit in a large bowl, toss, then set aside. Take the package of vanilla instant pudding and sprinkle about 2 tablespoons powder on top of the fruit. Toss it gently. Add 1½ teaspoons of vanilla and toss gently. Put in the fridge for 2 hours to chill. Take out, toss gently, and serve.

No Fail Lemon Pie

~

This is my favorite recipe from one of my favorite books. I was browsing through a thrift store and came across a book by Marjorie Pay Hinckley. This recipe was included. If I ever get to heaven, she is one of the first people I will want to meet. Besides being a lovely person, her lemon pie is truly fail proof.

This recipe had ten thousand likes on my TikTok and 867 shares. I hope everyone liked it as much as I do.

Ingredients

6 level tablespoons of flour
6 level tablespoons of cornstarch
1 cup sugar
2 pinches salt
3 cups water
4 egg yolks
3 lemons

Instructions

Spray the bottom of a medium-sized pot with non-stick cooking oil. Add flour, cornstarch, sugar, salt, and water. Boil continuously for ten minutes, stirring often. Beat egg yolks and stir into boiling mixture. It will turn a beautiful yellow color. Grate the rind of lemons and squeeze the juice, then add to the pie-filling mixture. Stir well. Cool and spoon into ready-baked crust. This is a nice addition to a company dinner. They will think you worked over the stove for hours.

Oatmeal Bread

Ingredients

3 bananas

2 cups oatmeal

2 eggs

¼ cup brown sugar

1 teaspoon baking soda

Instructions

Preheat oven at 350°F. Mix all together. Pour into baking pan and bake for 30 minutes.

Ogden Temple Carrot Cookies

~

This recipe came from an old recipe book that belonged to my mother-in-law. I remember her making these cookies, but I never knew the name until I found it many years later. Here's a great way to get your kids to eat carrots!

Ingredients

¾ cup sugar
¾ cup shortening
1 egg
1 cup cooked, mashed carrots
2 cups flour
2 teaspoons baking powder
1 teaspoon salt
1 teaspoon vanilla
½ cup coconut
Powdered sugar
1 orange, zested and juiced

Instructions

Preheat oven to 375°F. Cream sugar, shortening, egg, and carrots. Sift dry ingredients and add to carrot mixture. Then add vanilla and coconut. Drop on greased cookie sheet and bake for 12 to 15 minutes.

Icing Instructions

Mix desired amount of powdered sugar, grated rind and juice of orange. Drizzle on cookies for thin icing or spread it with a knife if you prefer it to be thick.

Pat's Cookies

Pat is one of the most productive and actively engaged ninety-year-olds I have ever known in my life. She is my hero. She not only bakes delicious cookies but is also looking for ways to help others in any way she can. It's not surprising to see her walking down the sidewalk with her friend on any early morning.

This recipe is enough for a whole neighborhood. You might want to reduce it.

Ingredients

2 cups butter

2 cups sugar

2 cups brown sugar

4 eggs

2 teaspoons vanilla

4 cups flour

5 cups oatmeal

1 teaspoon salt

2 teaspoons baking powder

2 teaspoons baking soda

1 (24-ounce) chocolate chips

1 (24-ounce) white chocolate chips

1 cup shredded coconut

Nuts, if desired

Instructions

Preheat oven to 375°F. Cream sugar and butter. Add eggs and vanilla. Set aside. Mix all ingredients, then add to sugar mixture. Bake for 9 minutes.

Snowflake Ice Cream

~

This recipe was found in an old recipe book I picked up from a Goodwill. To me, it represents the simplicity that we have long lost. Imagine not being able to go to the store to buy ice cream. I'm not one who would like that . . .

Snow must be very deep, well frozen, not the soft, wet kind. Scrape off the surface and fill one or two buckets with dry white snow.

Ingredients

2 eggs, slightly beaten
¼ teaspoon salt
1 cup sugar
1 qt milk, scalded
1 teaspoon vanilla

Instructions

Combine eggs, salt, and sugar. Stir in milk and cook in a bain-marie or double boiler for 5 minutes, until mixture coats spoon. Stir constantly. Add vanilla and cool to room temperature. While one person stirs vigorously, another adds the snow until it begins to freeze, and no more snow can be beaten in. Eat in a hurry. Children love its taste of "mittens and vanilla."

The Orange, Orange Stuff

~

I'm not certain where this recipe came from. I only know for sure that I have been preparing it for over fifty years. It's my husband's favorite, and it's protein packed (shhh . . . don't tell him it's healthy). The name is what he has always called it.

Most of the ingredients are left up to your taste and preference. However, this is our favorite.

Ingredients

2 large (15-ounce) cans mandarin oranges, drained well
2 large (20-ounce) cans pineapple chunks, drained well
1 8-ounce tub of Cool Whip
1 16-ounce tub of cottage cheese
1 large (6-ounce) packet orange Jell-O

Instructions

Blend cottage cheese and Cool Whip. Fold in packet of Jell-O. Add fruit. Chill. This keeps for several days in the fridge.

Affirmations

Affirmations

~

I will move beyond my fears.

My best is yet to come.

I am endlessly creating a new me.

I love myself unconditionally.

I will make peace with my past.

I have faith in myself.

I deserve the best in life.

I am strong.

I am confident.

I will believe in me.

I am doing my best and that is all I can do.

My best is good enough.

I will not let others define me.

I am enough.

I CAN DO HARD THINGS!

And. I. Love. You.

About the Author

~

I am Grandmagreat, wife to the man who loves me in spite of me. We have been married almost 57 lovely, sometimes very tumultuous, and always challenging years. We have five beautiful, imperfect but perfectly wonderful children. They have brought us 16 beautiful grandchildren who in turn, so far, have blessed us with 10 perfect great-grandchildren.

I am a college student, avid reader, poet, storyteller, and people lover. Interacting with my 3.3 million Tik-Tok "grandchildren" can only be described as pure joy! My passion (along with everything else) is finding "simply delicious" recipes from old recipe books and sharing the preparation with my beautiful TikTok grandchildren.

I love God. I am busy with more energy than I deserve,

Photo Credit Matthew West

and I don't plan on slowing down anytime soon. I love elephants, butterflies, sunflowers, angels, and most of all, people everywhere. I believe laughing is the best therapy ever. "I can do hard things," and I believe in helping others to have that belief as well. Giving time, effort and love to as many people as you can every single day, creates inner peace and happiness.

www.ingramcontent.com/pod-product-compliance
Lightning Source LLC
Chambersburg PA
CBHW020408150626
46554CB00012B/415